TRAFFIC LAW ENFORCEMENT

TRAFFIC LAW ENFORCEMENT

By

DONALD J. BASHAM
*Sergeant, California Highway Patrol
Instructor, Traffic Law and Accident Investigation
College of the Redwoods
Eureka, California*

HV
8079.5
.B37

CHARLES C THOMAS • PUBLISHER
Springfield • Illinois • U.S.A.

Published and Distributed Throughout the World by
CHARLES C THOMAS • PUBLISHER
BANNERSTONE HOUSE
301-327 East Lawrence Avenue, Springfield, Illinois, U.S.A.

This book is protected by copyright. No part of it
may be reproduced in any manner without written
permission from the publisher.

© *1978, by* CHARLES C THOMAS • PUBLISHER
ISBN 0-398-03772-8
Library of Congress Catalog Card Number: 77-26971

With THOMAS BOOKS *careful attention is given to all details of manufacturing and design. It is the Publisher's desire to present books that are satisfactory as to their physical qualities and artistic possibilities and appropriate for their particular use.* THOMAS BOOKS *will be true to those laws of quality that assure a good name and good will.*

Printed in the United States of America
N-11

Library of Congress Cataloging in Publication Data

Basham, Donald J
   Traffic law enforcement.

  Includes index.
  1. Traffic police.   2. Traffic regulations.
I. Title.
HV8079.5.B37   363.2'33   77-26971
ISBN 0-398-03772-8

TO

My wife, Mary, for her encouragement and love.

PREFACE

THIS TEXT is not intended to be a dry, technical manual. It does provide some specific data and can be used as a reference. It was written with the idea of sharing information about the police traffic control function which has come from years of street experience as well as hundreds of hours in the classroom.

The author is a college instructor in the subjects of traffic law and accident investigation. The material in the text is directly from classroom lectures and discussion sessions with other officers.

It is the author's opinion that traffic control is a science which may be applied anywhere in the world using the same principles and techniques. The text is deliberately nonlocalized, although California is the place from which the experiences and knowledge came. California has more vehicles on its highways than does any other area in the world. California has the complete variety of traffic ranging from super-sophisticated freeways which are patrolled by helicopter and monitored by closed circuit TV cameras activated by sensors imbedded in the roadbed to the two-lane dirt road in the county.

The principles espoused in the following chapters are believed to be as relevant in Europe as in California, as well as in New York City, Montreal, Sidney, or anywhere.

The common denominator of traffic control is the human behavior in a predictable pattern. It was the motive behind this book to provide human expertise to deal with human problems.

If the contents of this text are read as though the reader were listening to a squad room story session or a classroom lecture on a subject that is important to him, the book will speak to him and the meaning will hopefully be clear.

CONTENTS

Preface .... *Page* vii

Chapter
1. WORDS AND PHRASES DEFINED 3
2. THE POLICE TRAFFIC CONTROL FUNCTION ... 11
3. PRELIMINARY PROCEDURES FOR TRAFFIC STOPS 26
4. ENFORCEMENT TACTICS AND SAFETY DURING A TRAFFIC STOP 36
5. HANDLING VIOLATORS DURING A TRAFFIC STOP 47
6. EXAMINING IDENTIFICATION DOCUMENTS 52
7. AUTOMOTIVE EQUIPMENT INSPECTION 56
8. APPREHENDING SPEED VIOLATORS 64
9. EMERGENCY VEHICLE OPERATION 71
10. RECOGNIZING COMMON DRIVING VIOLATIONS OBSERVED DURING PATROL 79
11. FELONY STOPS AND ROADBLOCKS 91
12. INTOXICATED DRIVER DETECTION 103
13. INTOXICATED DRIVER ARREST PROCEDURE .. 117
14. INTOXICATED DRIVER ARREST REPORTS 126
15. COURT TESTIMONY 135

Appendix 141
Index 161

TRAFFIC LAW ENFORCEMENT

CHAPTER ONE

WORDS AND PHRASES DEFINED

IT IS NECESSARY, for the purpose of clarity, that a definition be established for certain words, phrases, and terms that are used in this text. The definitions which are listed in this chapter are intended to insure unity of understanding when the items are encountered in following chapters. It is also the intent of the author to promote the use of these words, phrases, and terms by traffic officers when writing their reports and when testifying in court. The student of traffic law enforcement is a student of a scientific process which requires uniformity of reference.

When the words, phrases, or terms appear in later chapters, it is recommended that the reader turn back to this part of the book and read again the specific meaning of the item. Then its use will make sense and the message will hopefully become clear.

ACCIDENT (TRAFFIC): An unintentional event which involves property damage or personal injury as the result of a vehicle in motion.

ACCIDENT PROBABILITY CHART: A graphic illustration of the projection of accident statistics in such a manner as to predict the pattern and frequency of future accidents for the purpose of preventive deployment of law enforcement personnel.

AIR BRAKES: A brake system which uses compressed air to actuate the service brakes at the wheels of a vehicle or as a power source for controlling or applying service brakes which are actuated through hydraulic or other intermediate means.

ALCOHOL: A colorless, volatile, flammable liquid (C_2H_5OH) that is the intoxicating agent in fermented and distilled liquors.

ALLEY: Any highway, having a roadway which does not exceed 25 feet in width, that is primarily used for access to the rear or side entrances of abutting property (refer to Highway and Roadway in this chapter).

ARREST: The restriction of a person's movement or the detaining in custody by authority of law.

AUTHORIZED EMERGENCY VEHICLE: Any publicly owned vehicle used by police, firefighters, ambulance, or rescue crews for the purpose of responding to a reported emergency.

AXLE: A structure consisting of one or more shafts, spindles, or bearings in the same vertical transverse plane by means of which, in conjunction with wheels mounted on said shafts, spindles, or bearings, a portion of the weight of the vehicle is continuously transmitted to the roadway.

BICYCLE: A mechanical device which may be mounted by a person and propelled exclusively by human power through a belt, chain, or gears and having either two or three wheels in a tandem or tricycle arrangement.

BLOOD/ALCOHOL LEVEL: A form of measurement which determines the volume of alcohol in a person's bloodstream by means of chemical analysis.

BUS: A motor vehicle designed to accommodate more than ten seated persons and used or maintained for the transportation of passengers.

BUSINESS DISTRICT: Roadside property, of which a preponderant ratio consists of buildings occupied and in use for business purposes.

CAMPER: A structure designed to be mounted upon a motor vehicle and to provide facilities for human habitation or camping purposes.

CROSSWALK (MARKED): Any portion of a roadway which is distinctly indicated for pedestrian use by means of lines or markings on the pavement surface.

CROSSWALK (UNMARKED): The prolongation of the boundary lines of a sidewalk at a junction where two roadways intersect at approximately right angles.

CUSTODY: Immediate charge and control exercised by a person in authority.

DARKNESS: The time period from one-half hour after sunset to one-half hour before sunrise or any time when visibility is so limited that a person or object cannot be clearly discerned at a distance of 1000 feet.

DISPATCHER: The base station radio operator of a police or fire department who notifies mobile field units of requests for service and information related to emergencies and acts as a central communications figure.

DRIVER: The person occupying or mounted upon a vehicle who has actual physical control of the vehicle and the capability to control its movement.

DRIVER'S LICENSE: Permission in writing to drive a specified type of motor vehicle or combination of vehicles, issued by the authority having jurisdiction.

DRUG: Any substance or combination of substances, *other than alcohol*, which, if ingested, would impair the psychomotor functions of a human being.

DRUNK: See Intoxication.

D.W.I.: Driving while intoxicated.

EMERGENCY: A situation which involves an immediate threat to persons or property, or an event still in progress in which injury or damage has occurred.

EMERGENCY VEHICLE: See Authorized emergency vehicle.

ESSENTIAL PARTS: All integral and body parts of a vehicle, the removal, alteration, or substitution of which would tend to conceal the identity of the vehicle or substantially alter its appearance.

FENDER: A guard over the wheel of a vehicle which serves to reduce the spray of water, mud, and debris encountered in the roadway.

FIFTH WHEEL: A coupling device used to connect two vehicles, which consists of an upper and lower skid plate, a king pin, coupler jaws, or similar parts designed and arranged in such a way as to be readily separable, permit free rotation between the upper and lower halves, and provide lateral stability to the towed vehicle.

FIXED POST: A term which refers to the assignment of a traffic officer to a specific location for traffic control purposes.

FLAMMABLE LIQUID: Any liquid which has a flash point (closed cup test) below 200 degrees Fahrenheit and a vapor pressure not in excess of 26 PSI gauge at a temperature of 100 degrees Fahrenheit.

FLARE PATTERN: The design which is formed by lighted fusees placed on the roadway in such a manner as to outline the safest route past a hazard or to indicate no passage due to extreme hazard. Single fusees may be used to attract the attention of approaching traffic to a hazard about to be encountered.

FREEWAY: A highway which has no toll stations and which may be traveled by a motorist continuously for its entire length without encountering conflict with cross traffic.

FUSEE: A friction-ignited flare used as a signal to warn approaching traffic of a hazard.

HIGHWAY: A way or place of whatever nature, constructed and maintained at public expense, which is open to the use of the public for travel by motorists, bicyclists, equestrians, and pedestrians. This definition includes roads and streets.

HOUSE CAR: A motor vehicle which has been originally designed or permanently altered and equipped for human habitation or to which a camper has been attached.

ILLEGAL: Prohibited by law.

INJURY: Physical damage to a human being which may be indicated by a visible wound or complaint of pain.

INTERSECTION: The space contained within the lateral curb or boundary lines of the roadways of separate highways which join one another at any angle.

INTOXICATION: A condition characterized by diminished senses and psychomotor skills, usually the result of ingested alcohol, drugs, or a combination of both.

INVESTIGATION: A study by means of systematic inquiry which documents facts, physical evidence, and statements, as well as the opinions, conclusions, and recommendations of the investigator.

JURISDICTION: The limits within which legal authority may be exercised.

LIMIT LINE: A solid line extending across a roadway to indicate the point at which traffic is required to stop in compliance with legal requirements.

LOCAL AUTHORITIES: The legislative body of every county or municipality having authority to adopt local police regulations.

MANDATORY: Requiring compliance.

MAY: A word which offers permission. When used in the writing of the law it expresses allowance for a specified act.

MOTOR CARRIER: A company or individual who engages in the business of transporting persons or property on the highway.

MOTOR VEHICLE: A vehicle which is self-propelled.

MOTORCYCLE: A motor vehicle, other than a tractor, which has a saddle for the rider and is designed to have not more than three wheels in contact with the roadway. A motorcycle that has a sidecar which causes the combined vehicles to have a maximum of four wheels in contact with the roadway is still defined as a motorcycle.

MUFFLER: An automotive device consisting of a series of chambers or baffle plates or other mechanical design, for the purpose of receiving exhaust gas from an internal combustion engine, is effective in reducing engine noise.

MUST: Requiring compliance.

ODOMETER: An instrument installed in a motor vehicle which indicates the distance traveled by the vehicle.

OFFICER: A police employee who has legal powers of arrest and authority to regulate public conduct through the enforcement of laws.

OFFICIAL TRAFFIC CONTROL DEVICE: Any sign, signal, marking, or device placed or erected for the purpose of regulating, warning, or guiding traffic by authority of a public body or official having jurisdiction.

OFFICIAL TRAFFIC CONTROL SIGNAL: Any device, manually, electrically, or mechanically operated, by which traffic is alternately directed to stop and proceed and which is erected by authority or a public body or official having jurisdiction.

PARK OR PARKING: The standing of a vehicle, whether occupied or not, except for the temporary purpose of and while actually engaged in the loading or unloading of passengers.

PEDESTRIAN: Any person who is afoot or who is using a means of conveyance propelled by human power other than a bicycle.

PNEUMATIC TIRE: A tire which is capable of inflation with compressed air.

POWER BRAKES: Any mechanism that aids in applying the brakes of a vehicle by means of vacuum, compressed air, or electricity.

PRIVATE ROAD: A way or place in private ownership designated for vehicular travel by the owner and those having express permission or implied permission by the owner.

RADAR: An electronic device used by traffic law enforcement officers to measure the speed of moving vehicles.

RECONSTRUCTED VEHICLE: A vehicle which has been materially altered from its original construction by the removal, addition, or substitution of essential parts, new or used.

REGISTERED OWNER: The one who is officially recorded as the owner of a vehicle. It may be the same as the legal owner or in addition to the legal owner.

REGISTRATION: The official document which identifies a vehicle through the Vehicle Identification Number (VIN) and a description including the year, make, and model, as well as the name and address of the registered and legal owners.

RESIDENTIAL DISTRICT: Roadside property, of which a preponderate ratio consists of buildings occupied and in use as private dwellings.

RIGHT-OF-WAY: The privilege of the immediate use of the highway.

ROADWAY: That portion of a highway improved, designed, or ordinarily used for vehicular travel.

SEMITRAILER: A vehicle used in conjunction with a motor vehicle, so designed that a portion of its weight and that of its load is supported by another vehicle when coupled for towing.

SIDEWALK: That portion of a highway, other than the roadway, set apart by curbs, barriers, markings, or other delineation for pedestrian travel.

SIREN: A device, either electrical or mechanical, which emits a wailing sound as a warning of the approach of an emergency vehicle.

SPECIALLY CONSTRUCTED VEHICLE: A vehicle not originally constructed under a distinctive name, make, model, or type by a generally recognized manufacturer of vehicles.

SPEED TRAP: A term used to describe the clandestine surveillance of traffic by an officer for the purpose of detecting and arresting speed law violators.

SPEEDOMETER: An instrument installed in a motor vehicle which indicates the speed of the vehicle while in motion.

SYNERGISTIC EFFECT: The joint action of agents so that their combined effect is greater than the algebraic sum of their individual effects.

TITLE: The official document which certifies clear ownership of a vehicle.

TOW TRUCK: A motor vehicle which has been altered or designed and equipped for and exclusively used in the business of towing vehicles by means of a crane, hoist, tow bar, tow line, or dolly.

TRAFFIC: Includes pedestrians, equestrians, driven animals, vehicles, and other conveyances while using the highway for the purpose of travel.

TRAFFIC CITATION: A written notice to appear in court issued by a traffic officer, resulting from an observed violation of law.

TRAFFIC COLLISION: An event in which personal injury or property damage results from the movement of a vehicle.

TRAFFIC OFFICER: Any peace officer on duty for the exclusive or main purpose of enforcing traffic regulations and facilitating the safe use of the highway.

TRAFFIC STOP: A term used to describe the official act of an officer in the detaining of a motorist in transit for the purpose of enforcement or investigation.

UNDER THE INFLUENCE: A condition of impairment which is the beginning stage of intoxication.

VEHICLE: A device by which persons or property may be transported upon a highway.

VEHICLE MOTION: The action of a vehicle which results in the traversing of a distance, however slight.

VEHICULAR CROSSING: A public bridge constructed over a body of water or other obstacle, which is designed, used, and maintained for vehicles in transit, usually for a toll.

VIN: Vehicle identification number. A serial number assigned to a vehicle at the factory for the purpose of identification, which conforms with the registration.

CHAPTER TWO

THE POLICE TRAFFIC CONTROL FUNCTION

THE MATERIAL in this chapter is intended to provide the reader with the necessary information to accomplish the following:
- Understand the standard police responsibility in controlling traffic
- Utilize the effect of police presence on the behavior of drivers and pedestrians to reduce accident frequency
- Prepare an accident probability chart
- Direct traffic by hand signal

Since the advent of the automobile, it has been the inherited responsibility of the police to control its movement. After the first traffic accident occurred early in this century, it became apparent that the need for control was based on safety. It follows that traffic law enforcement and traffic supervision are aimed at providing traffic safety. It has been proven that by studying the patterns of traffic accidents and compiling statistics, it is possible to predict their frequency and to approximate when and where they will occur. Using these probability data, the traffic officer can have a direct effect on the frequency of traffic accidents.

People who are driving motor vehicles have long ago associated the presence of a marked police vehicle in their vicinity with the possibility of receiving a traffic citation. Since traffic citations result usually in an expense in terms of both time and money, most motorists consciously wish to avoid receiving one; therefore, they adjust their driving habits accordingly when they believe there is the possibility of being the recipient of enforcement action by a police officer. Armed with this information, traffic officers can have a particular effect on groups of drivers by the use of high visibility patrol in those areas which statistics indicate are frequent accident locations.

In the early days of traffic law enforcement, it quickly became the habit of the police in the United States to wait in ambush, out of sight, and pounce upon the unsuspecting motorist who had erred in his driving, usually by exceeding the speed limit. It was not long before this activity by the police became widely known and feared. In some localities the police, in conjunction with a local judge, ran a revenue-producing business which quickly received the title of "speed trap." The speed trap was set up in a location where motorists were known to drive at speeds usually higher than the limit. In some cases, speed limits were posted which were lower than necessary in order that more speeders could be apprehended, and revenue became the main motivating factor. The technique which was used involved a traffic officer on a motorcycle parked behind a billboard or some other obstacle which concealed his presence. He then had clear visibility of the roadway but was not readily visible to the drivers on the highway. One method that gained popularity among officers involved in this activity was the use of a stopwatch to time the passing of an automobile between two points, thereby determining its speed. This activity became so distasteful to so many people that laws have been passed in some parts of the United States prohibiting the operation of a speed trap; in other locations, its use continues. These techniques and others will be discussed in more detail in a later chapter on speed enforcement.

The monitoring and supervision of driver conduct on public highways will continue to be a standard police responsibility in civilized nations. Some police agencies, especially larger ones, have established a separate division which is specifically specialized in the enforcement of traffic laws and the investigation of traffic collisions. In other agencies, quite often smaller ones, it is the duty of the generalist patrolman to include traffic law enforcement and traffic supervision in his daily beat patrol. Unfortunately, due to other responsibilities and distractions, the generalist patrolman is not able to concentrate sufficient time and energy on traffic control to make a significant change in traffic patterns and have a lasting effect on accident frequencies. The presence of his marked police vehicle and the sight of his roadside encounter with an occasional motorist do have a "halo effect" on other drivers at least for a brief period after they pass his location. In some cases, it is because the driver is a conscientious citizen and is reminded by having seen the officer engaged in traffic enforcement that his own driving habits require his full attention. Others who are not as concerned with obedience to the law will react to the roadside activities of a police officer out of fear that they too will be the recipients of a traffic citation.

Because of this reaction of the motoring public to an officer engaged in roadside contact with a motorist, it is desirable that officers make this contact as often as possible. It is not necessary each time a traffic officer stops a vehicle for a minor infraction that he issue a traffic citation. Often, an officer may be engaged in notifying a motorist of a nonhazardous defect in his automotive equipment. The officer may also be engaged in giving directions to some geographical location. The purpose of the stop is not known to those motorists who are driving past. It is often the automatic assumption by observing motorists that the officer is issuing a traffic citation. Therefore, armed with this information, a traffic officer who makes frequent contact with motorists at the roadside is creating a "halo effect" on the traffic in his immediate vicinity and is accomplishing his mission, to have a positive effect on traffic safety.

There have been extensive studies conducted by major law enforcement agencies in the United States on the effect of visible police patrol in high crime areas. The purpose was to determine if the presence of uniformed police officers on foot and in clearly marked vehicles would have a deterrent effect on crime in specific locations. The results of these studies have indicated that the majority of the time police presence had little or no effect on the occurrence of crime. This revelation was very disturbing to police administrators in general who were at a loss to understand why this is so. These results also made it difficult to justify the cost of large patrol divisions. It is the author's opinion that the reason for this negative result was because many crimes occur behind closed doors and quite often as the result of spontaneous behavior as in the case of aggravated assaults and some homicides. It is true that a burglar or a mugger looking for a target victim should be deterred from his pursuits by the presence of a uniformed officer. However, because the officer must usually have sufficient cause to believe that the individual is engaged in criminal actions before making a stop or detaining the individual, this deterrent effect is limited. Individuals who are engaged in premeditative crimes usually have experience in dealing with police and are aware of police procedure. Therefore, the presence of uniformed officers in the area does not necessarily affect the activity of these people.

Traffic violations are a different matter. The presence of marked traffic enforcement vehicles in areas of high accident frequency does have a deterrent effect on the unsafe driving habits of motorists. A police department can make effective use of traffic accident statistics to deploy traffic officers in areas of high accident frequency. When the data are properly analyzed, traffic control supervisors can brief their officers with the time, location, and type of violation which causes the majority of accidents in a given area. It will take some courage at first for a traffic sergeant to remove his men entirely from some areas which do not show a high accident frequency and concentrate them in the area which does have an accident problem. By this saturation process, the traffic officers create the illusion of omnipresence for the motorists in the area. Frequent roadside contacts with those motorists will have a definite effect on the occurrence of traffic accidents.

The best known tool for the traffic supervisor to determine where these locations are and when and where to deploy his traffic officers is a device known as a probability chart. The probability chart is a result of study and selective review of accident information. First, a significant period of time must be sampled in order to establish a dominant pattern. Human beings who operate vehicles usually follow a predictable pattern in their driving. These patterns are quite often related to seasons of the year. Therefore, the months of the year need to be compared with the same months of previous years to be meaningful. An example of this is comparison of January only with January of previous years (usually no less than three years in a row) as opposed to comparing January with August. January, being a midwinter month, may have the accident-producing weather of wintertime, i.e. slippery roads from ice and snow, etc., which causes a higher rate of accidents than August. The twelve months of the year, if compared with the same months in a three-to-five-year period (depending upon the availability of records), could be used to develop probability charts.

The primary factors necessary to construct a probability chart are where the accidents are occurring and when they are occurring. The "where" factor means both the beat number and specific locations within that beat. However, to keep the chart simple, the beat number will suffice. The "when" factor means time of day and day of week. The causes of the accidents may be of interest to the traffic supervisor and to the officers, but cause is not a necessary factor in order for the probability chart to be effective. When a piece of graph paper is used to create a twenty-four-hour clock and blocks are drawn in to represent time periods, a diagram can be created to show at a glance what days of the week and what times of the day are problems on what beats. With this information, the traffic supervisor can deploy his officers on a daily basis to achieve maximum effectiveness in deterring unsafe driving conduct by motorists in the area.

It should be the practice of traffic officers assigned to an area where accidents are occurring to make traffic stops on any and all observed violations regardless of how minor they may be. It was stated earlier that a traffic citation need not be issued on each and every occasion. However, a stop should be made and the contact established. The officer's own experience and judgement will dictate when a traffic citation is appropriate. It may be desirable for a police chief to establish an enforcement policy to guide officers in uniformly enforcing the traffic laws. However, it is recommended that traffic officers be allowed a considerable

16   *Traffic Law Enforcement*

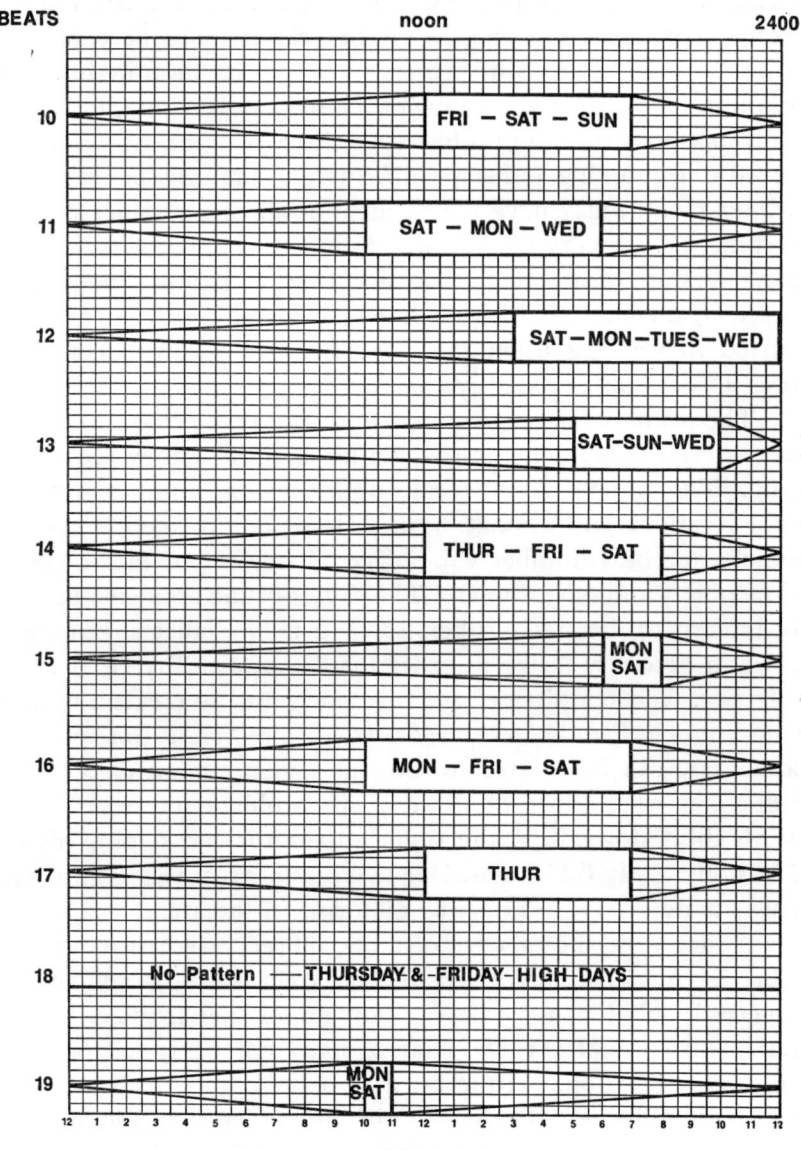

Figure 1.

degree of discretion and flexibility in this regard. If this procedure is followed strictly, a decline in traffic accident frequency will be assured. This has been proven on numerous occasions in controlled experiments.

Highly motivated traffic officers were used to follow the probability chart, and when the deployment was based on this information and when the officers were aggressive in making frequent contact with motorists on the beats involved, the number of traffic accidents decreased dramatically. It was also determined during the experiment that the morale of the traffic officers involved in the project was improved because they understood what they were doing and they could see the results of their efforts. This side benefit of job satisfaction among traffic officers is a bonus for any police administrator who also has the measurable results from the efforts of those satisfied officers.

Directing traffic is a part of the traffic control function, and it is both an art and a science. It is an art from the standpoint that it requires a certain amount of human creativity in providing guidance for others and changing chaos to order. It is a science because it involves applying specific rules which will produce predictable results.

A traffic officer may be required to direct traffic as part of his regular duties. It may be necessary on a scheduled basis for an officer to control the movement of vehicles and pedestrians at a specific location on a daily shift. The other occasions when directing traffic is required will probably be either at an accident scene or the scene of some other disaster, including a fire. Quite often the fire department will require this type of assistance from the police. It usually involves diverting traffic around the scene and, when possible, avoiding the emergency equipment parked in the vicinity.

Planned recreational events, such as football games and other large gatherings of the public will require police traffic direction. Usually these events are scheduled in advance and a plan determined by the police department as to the method of traffic direction. Quite often in these situations, due to the large number of vehicles and persons, more than one officer will be required to control one location. When this occurs, it is imperative that the two officers work together as a team in order not to cause a problem worse than the original.

One of the most important tools of a traffic officer when involved in traffic direction is the whistle. It is not possible to overemphasize the importance of this item. All too often traffic officers will attempt to direct traffic silently while using only arm and hand gestures, but having no verbal contact with the drivers or pedestrians. The human voice is not the appropriate device to use for controlling groups of people, especially when they are inside of vehicles. If it were practical to amplify the voice of the officer through a public address system so that he could speak directly to drivers and pedestrians, it might be sufficient. However, the unique sound of the traffic whistle will usually be audible through the din of automotive noise and other sounds which surround an intersection; it is distinctive and it penetrates. The traffic whistle also provides the officer with the ability to be heard and to be recognized.

A skillful traffic officer who uses his whistle often enough to become familiar with its tone characteristics can communicate as effectively through the tones produced from the whistle as he can by speaking directly to an individual.

It is essential in directing traffic by hand to establish eye contact with specific drivers in order to be assured that the gestures are recognized. When eye contact is established and the whistle used, total communication will very likely be established.

Earlier it was stated that directing traffic is an art. This art form is individualized when the officer develops his own style in terms of body language and other communication during the function of directing traffic by hand. The use of the traffic whistle is definitely a part of this. It is as though the whistle were a musical instrument through which feelings and thoughts could be expressed from one human being to another.

The whistle also provides a command presence and an official status which is usually readily accepted by the motoring public. The sound of the police whistle is recognized around the world, and the normal response is to comply with the directions of the officer. He is removed from the status of just another human being and placed in that special category of "police officer."

The officer will develop his own format, to some extent, in using the whistle to communicate. However, uniformity throughout as large an area as possible is desirable in order to assure compliance. When stopping traffic, a long, continuous blast on the whistle will usually draw attention and communicate the intention to stop traffic. When starting traffic from a standstill, two short, staccato bursts are used, accompanied by appropriate hand motions, in order to start the traffic moving. When an individual motorist or pedestrian is moving contrary to the flow of traffic or to the officer's directions, it will be necessary to obtain that person's attention. One of the best ways to do that is with the whistle. A series of half a dozen or so short, staccato bursts will usually do the trick. The sound is similar to that of a scolding bluejay. Once the officer has obtained eye contact with the errant driver, he may then reestablish order by gesturing to that person where he wants him to go.

Hand signals in traffic direction should be simple and consistent. It is desirable, especially when directing traffic for a long period, to wear white gloves in order to accentuate the hands. If the officer's uniform is dark in color, the white gloves will stand out even more and make it easy for the officer to use hand movements to catch the eye of persons in traffic. It is naturally desirable for an officer who is directing traffic to be in full uniform. This makes it easy for those drivers and pedestrians who are to be controlled to recognize the authority of the officer, and it will usually elicit willing compliance. If it is necessary in an emergency for an officer not in uniform to direct traffic, an effort should be made to display his badge in a conspicuous location on his clothing. Most people will comply with the directions of a person who obviously knows what he is doing, and this is needed sometimes at accident scenes when civilians assist an officer by diverting traffic. However, if drivers see the badge as the symbol of authority and recognize that the person is a policeman, they will most likely comply more willingly.

The body language of a traffic officer is very important and accompanies the hand gestures as well as the use of the whistle, providing a total form of communication. When traffic is flowing in a two-way direction, the officer should stand with his sides toward the direction of travel and his front and back toward stopped traffic. The reason for this is to provide a larger surface to be observed by traffic that must stop; when they see the front or back of the officer, especially if this practice is followed uniformly, they will know that they should stop. Most people will be watching the officer closely, waiting for him to gesture his desire as to which way they should go. The practical aspect of standing with one's sides to flowing traffic is that of providing a smaller target and being less likely to be struck by a passing car.

When the flow of traffic is to be stopped, if it is two way, the officer should raise both hands in opposite directions with the palms facing the oncoming traffic and produce a long, loud, continuous burst from the whistle in order to establish audible contact as well as visual. He should continue to stand with the hands raised until all traffic has come to a complete stop. Then, with the hands still in the extended position, he should turn his body so that he is now facing stopped traffic and his sides are toward that traffic which he is about to move. With the palms still extended, indicating that he wishes them to remain stopped until he is ready, the officer points toward the lead vehicles. He should establish eye contact with those drivers and produce two short bursts on the whistle as he simultaneously gestures for them to move forward. The most clearly visible means of hand signal in this movement will be to allow the elbow to act as a fulcrum with the arms extended straight out from the body, rotating the hand and forearm in a circular motion from the elbow and drawing the traffic forward. This movement is not only highly visible but also gives the officer an alert appearance. People respond very well to an officer who is alert and professional in his appearance. Anyone who has ever observed an officer directing traffic in a sloppy manner, looking very bored by what he is doing and perhaps gesturing from the wrist only, will know what I mean. Long periods of directing traffic in the proper manner will produce definite fatigue because the arms are raised so much. This is one of the reasons why it is important for an officer to be in good physical condition and able to maintain a fixed-post traffic control for an extended period of time.

When traffic has passed in sufficient volume for the officer to change directions again, the same procedure is followed by raising the arms, extending the palms flat toward oncoming traffic, and producing a long, continuous burst from the whistle to notify that traffic to stop. Then, turning the body so that the front and back are toward the now stopped lanes, the officer again establishes eye contact with the lead drivers, points to them, produces two short, loud bursts on the whistle, and rotates the hands and forearms smartly in the direction that the drivers are to go. Normally, the officer will gesture for one lane to be passing by bringing his hand down smartly in front of his face and continuing on around again, indicating that the traffic is to pass in front of him on that side. For the traffic that will pass to his rear, the motion should be made behind the head to indicate that they are to proceed on that side of his body.

When an approaching motorist indicates by signal that he wishes to make a left turn and such turn is permitted and practical, the officer should acknowledge his signal directly to the driver and then point to a spot on the pavement very near to the officer. This is intended to indicate that the driver should come to that location and stop until further notice. One additional hand signal that may be quickly added to this combination after pointing to the driver and pointing to the spot in the road is that of just briefly showing the palm of the hand to indicate that he is to stop at that point. Once the officer is sure that the driver is responding to his directions, he may then continue to devote his attention to the flow of traffic. When the officer sees an opportunity for the driver to safely turn left, he should then turn back toward him, establish eye contact, point directly at the driver, and gesture with the pointing finger in a circular motion indicating that the turn may now be completed. This is done again by pointing in the direction that the driver is to go. These gestures may be repeated several times in order to assure understanding. To be safe when allowing a driver to turn left, even though there may be a sufficient gap in oncoming opposite traffic, the traffic officer should raise his palm in that direction in case a car approaches which he has not seen while he is allowing a left turn. The raised palm will indicate to that driver that he is to stop and will most likely avoid a collision.

When a traffic officer assumes command of an intersection or location and begins to direct traffic by hand, he assumes all responsibility for the movement of traffic within that area. His mind must become computerlike in assessing the needs of the traffic and making sure that he does not direct vehicles in conflict with each other. It is possible to produce a very serious traffic accident by not being sure before moving traffic in more than one direction at a time.

Once again, when several officers are working on a location, it is essential that they cooperate and establish a harmonious rhythm in the movement of traffic in that location. Normally the easiest way to establish this is for one officer to take the lead and the other officer to follow that lead in determining when traffic will move and when it will stop. The lead officer assesses the overall situation and decides which traffic to start and how long to allow it to flow. When he is ready to change to a different pattern, he should establish eye contact with his partner, nod his head or in some other way indicate this indication of an upcoming change, then hold up his hands to notify drivers of the change in the flow and make sure that his partner is following suit. It is also possible to keep in touch with each other by previously agreed upon signals with the whistle which will communicate the intentions from one officer to another.

Different traffic situations will require different types of hand movements or body movements in order to control traffic. This is why an officer must be flexible and innovative when assessing a traffic situation which requires his control. It is very easy for an officer to become robotlike when confined to one location for a long period of time and responsible for the movement of a long, seemingly endless line of cars. However, for the officer's own mental health and the continuous need for public relations, it is important that he or she look at the people inside of the vehicles that are being directed. Quite often he will be rewarded by a sympathetic smile from an appreciative motorist who recognizes that without the officer's expert control at that location, he or she would probably be tied up in a hopeless traffic jam. These little smiles and expressions will go a long way in perking up the officer's morale, especially when he is hot and tired. It is a small item, but it makes the officer feel appreciated and important, and everyone needs that. Another reason for being aware of the occupants of vehicles as they pass is in order not to miss the opportunity to communicate with children. It is very important to a free and orderly society that children do not fear police. Rather, it is desirable that they respect and admire a police officer so that if they are lost or in need, they will not hesitate to approach an officer for assistance. This is very definitely a parental responsibility, but the officer has his responsibility also, to establish contact with children as often as possible and exhibit a friendly manner which will encourage them to communicate. Adults in any crowd will be pleased to see a police officer being kind to a child. The nurturing parent in grown-ups is brought out when they observe this occurring. It softens them toward the officer and perhaps also toward others. When the officer sees a car approaching with children inside, he should make a point to smile and even to wave, if that is possible without disrupting hand gestures to other traffic. The effort will pay many dividends of which the officer personally may not be aware, but which will benefit a lot of people. It is probable that police officers all have a desire to work with people, otherwise they would not have entered their profession. So, why should the officer not take advantage of every opportunity to communicate in a friendly way with people around him?

It will sometimes be necessary to deny a motorist permission to turn or to go in a certain direction, and this will be irritating to that motorist most of the time. Even though the officer may be tired and irritable from a long period of standing on the pavement, he should resist the temptation to become angry when motorists attempt to take advantage of his good nature or just slip by when he is not looking. The officer should remain firm, make his gestures clear, and emphasize them with the whistle. This will draw attention to the errant motorist and quite often he or she will feel the peer pressure to come in to line and comply as others are doing. Essentially, the power of the police officer comes from the people themselves, and without their willingness for the officer to be in control, he certainly would not be able to maintain it.

When directing traffic at night, it is essential that the officer be seen by approaching motorists. If the location is not well lighted, there are several ways to accomplish this. One way is to stand within a circle of lighted flares. The glow from the flames will illuminate the officer and also establish that an emergency situation exists. If the officer is going to be at the location for an extended period of time, it may be necessary to "stack" the flares in order for them to be self-lighting and provide a longer period of uninterrupted traffic control.

Another way for the officer to establish his presence in the dark is with the use of the flashlight. When the approach of headlights is observed and the officer wishes to establish visual contact with the oncoming motorists, the flashlight can be used to attract their attention and establish the presence of the officer. This can be done by shining the light directly at the oncoming vehicle and manipulating the wrist back and forth rapidly, causing a flashing effect. It is not likely that the hand-held flashlight will blind the oncoming motorists until they are very close, so there is no need to be concerned about shining the light directly at them while they are still at the distance of half a block or more. Once the officer is sure that the oncoming motorist sees him, the flashlight can be used as an extension of the hands and the arm moved in an exaggerated motion which is the same basic movement as used in the daylight. The person will see the moving of the light and recognize the intention. A red plastic cone attached to the head of the flashlight will glow with the beam and be more visible as the arm moves. Reflectorized tape can also be attached to the flashlight or to the back of gloves in order to pick up the headlight beam and make the motions more easily visible. Directing traffic is a dangerous activity at all times, but it is particularly dangerous in the darkness, and an officer must be extremely alert and ready to take evasive action to avoid being struck by passing traffic.

When directing traffic at an accident scene, particularly at night, the traffic officer must be alert for drivers who are distracted by the scene itself. The scene of a traffic accident, especially one with major damage, will draw the curiosity of passing motorists and may interfere with their observation of the officer directing traffic. This can be a dangerous situation when the motorist does not see the officer. It is also possible that the motorist may fail to see some hazard in the roadway that has not been removed while "rubbernecking" in the aftermath of the accident. Again, this is a situation which calls for vigorous use of the police whistle to obtain the undivided attention of approaching traffic.

In summary, fixed-post traffic direction can be an enjoyable part of the traffic control function of a police officer. It is the situation in which he works directly with people, providing a continuous service by expediting the flow of traffic and minimizing delay. He is further serving by assuring that safety prevails. Directing traffic can be hard, tedious work, but if the officer follows the guidelines contained within this chapter and allows himself to enjoy his work, he will find it to be a very rewarding part of his duties.

CHAPTER THREE

PRELIMINARY PROCEDURES FOR TRAFFIC STOPS

THE MATERIAL in this chapter is intended to provide the reader with the necessary information to accomplish the following:
- Plan a traffic stop in advance
- Obtain maximum effectiveness from the emergency lights
- Obtain maximum effectiveness from the siren
- Obtain maximum effectiveness from the public address system
- Position the patrol vehicle for maximum protection to the officer.

When an officer determines that he will stop a vehicle in traffic for the purpose of enforcement or investigation, he must begin to formulate a plan for the stop. He must survey the traffic conditions and the type of terrain adjacent to the highway where the stop will be made. If the stop is to be made at night, lighting conditions must also be considered. It is to the officer's advantage to make the stop in a well-lighted area where he can see the activities of the persons within the violator's vehicle as well as being seen by other motorists passing by. In the event that he needs backup assistance, it will be easier for the additional units to locate the officer if he is in a well-lighted area. Should the situation develop into an altercation between the officer and the violator, he will be more likely to attract attention from passing motorists if they can see the struggle taking place and in turn notify assistance.

If the stop is to be made in a downtown area or a neighborhood where there are buildings, the officer may wish to utilize the side of a building as a barrier to flight by foot if the violator attempts to run away.

If there are crowds of people in the area where the stop is to be made and they are likely to be hostile to the officer or interfere with the stop, he may wish to continue to roll for a short distance until he is out of that particular area before signaling the violator to pull over.

Some departments require their officers to notify the dispatcher by radio prior to making a traffic stop. This notification usually includes the location of the stop, a description of the vehicle and its license plates, and the basic reason for the stop (traffic only versus felony situation). This information may be useful in recognizing a potential problem and sending backup assistance to an officer in advance, or when he requests backup, to already have knowledge of his location for a speedy response. If the officer is injured or killed, there are data available from this transmission so that other officers will have a place to begin looking for the parties responsible. Unfortunately, the license plates do not always match the vehicle, and at night vehicle colors are difficult to determine accurately, especially under artificial lights. Therefore, even though an officer has complied with the regulation, he may have provided little or no valid information for follow-up. It is also one additional thing for the officer to concentrate on when trying to watch the vehicle he is stopping, observe traffic, and make sure that he is ready to exit the car in case the driver starts back toward him, and it can be more of a detriment than an asset. Some large police departments which have high volumes of radio traffic do not require their units to notify the dispatcher of every traffic stop. It would be impossible for the frequencies to carry such a volume of transmissions. Exterior radio speakers in the grill of the patrol car allow the officer to monitor radio calls while on the roadside dealing with the violator, and he can answer if he is called. Some officers use a pad of paper to record the license number of each stop made during the shift. When they complete the stop, the license number is crossed off. Should the officer be killed, this pad would have, theoretically, one license number not crossed off which would obviously be the last one encountered.

Planning a traffic stop means doing so every time so that the officer does not feel comfortable unless he has a plan formulated prior to activating his emergency lights or signaling to the driver to pull over to the roadside. There are five points which consistently accompany a successful traffic stop:

1. Capability
2. Confidence
3. Communication
4. Control
5. Confinement

Consider these separately: (1) *Capability* — Mainly, the capability is conveyed by legal power. The law bestows upon the officer the power to detain in transit motorists who are in violation of the law for the purpose of investigation or enforcement. The officer's personal capability in carrying out his work is interrelated with the following point: (2) *Confidence* — If the officer is well trained and aware of his personal capabilities, he will exhibit an air of confidence which will reassure a citizen observing his actions that he is capable of doing his job. It may also deter a violator from attempting to resist arrest if the violator is aware that the officer is confident in his own abilities. (3) *Communication* — that is, the communication which occurs between the officer and the violator. It is important that the violator understand what the officer wants, beginning when the violator is signaled, either by emergency lights or hand signal, to pull his vehicle to the roadside, and extending through the roadside contact. Obviously, if a language barrier exists, the officer will not be able to communicate, but usually a lack of communication occurs on a more subtle level. Police officers who perform their duties day in and day out for many years become very used to the procedure that they follow in making traffic stops and issuing traffic citations. However, not all of the motoring public is aware of these procedures; when an officer uses abbreviated language, he does not always achieve communication. It is necessary that the officer observe the violator very closely for signs of understanding. If he sees that confusion exists, he needs to take steps to eliminate it, e.g. avoiding an overbearing or morally superior attitude toward the person.

(4) *Control* — a term which means that the officer decides and exercises his powers to limit what occurs during the roadside transaction. He requires the violator to either stand along the roadside with him while he issues the citation or to remain seated in his vehicle, whichever conditions dictate. However, he does not permit the violator to wander about or permit passengers in the violator's vehicle to get out and interfere in the transaction. Usually this control will take place through a minimum effort exerted by the officer if all of the previous points are in effect. The need for control may indeed become physical in some traffic stops. Certain persons will not only verbally but physically resist the officer's efforts to regulate their driving conduct. If the officer is to succeed, he must be prepared to use whatever force is reasonable, including, if necessary, physical force.

(5) *Confinement* — a term synonymous with arrest; the person arrested is usually *confined* in handcuffs and ultimately in a jail cell. On a roadside detention, it is important that the situation be confined to as small an area as possible for the officer to complete his business. This is usually a space containing the violator's vehicle and the patrol car. If the situation spills out of this area, the officer will no longer be in control. Thus the officer must establish his perimeter in his own mind in order to successfully confine the situation. If the violator or members of his party attempt to move outside of the perimeter which the officer has in mind, he must exercise his control and require them to remain within.

Emergency warning lamps mounted on a police patrol vehicle are in fact signals to traffic that the police officer operating the vehicle is demanding the right of way when they are lighted. Most jurisdictions have a law which requires the motorist, upon observing these lights in operation, to immediately drive to the side of the road and stop until the vehicle has passed. If the vehicle does not pass, but pulls in behind the motorist, he then knows that he is the subject of the officer's intentions. The lights additionally serve as a warning to other traffic that an unusual and possibly hazardous situation is occurring at the roadside and that they need to be more alert when passing by. If an officer is making a dangerous arrest, he will want his emergency lights to serve as beacons for responding assistance.

There will also be times when the emergency lights can create an attractive nuisance which becomes a traffic hazard if they are left on even after the vehicles are no longer a hazard to passing traffic. It is easy for an officer to leave his lights on while completing his traffic stop because when the vehicle pulls to the roadside he is usually anxious to get out of his car and make contact; this is not always wise. It is important for traffic safety to avoid unnecessary distractions to passing motorists. People are naturally curious, and their attention will be diverted to the roadside detention by the flashing lights. Unless it is necessary for them to see that the vehicles are stopped at that location, the situation may become a hazard. If motorists are not paying attention to their own driving, a traffic accident may result.

In addition, an officer needs to consider the safest possible location to make the stop and then, once clear of the roadway itself he needs to consider extinguishing the emergency lights unless he has a specific reason for leaving them in operation.

Sometimes officers making a traffic stop tend to crowd too close to the rear of the vehicle they are attempting to stop. This anxious aggressiveness is understandable, but it is not safe. Two things may occur if the officer is following too closely when he attempts to make the stop. First, if the motorist is excitable and reacts too suddenly, the patrol vehicle may become involved in a rear-end collision. Second, if the patrol car is too close, the violator's rearview mirror may frame out emergency lights that are mounted on the roof of the patrol car. He may be vaguely aware of a colored glow from the emergency lights, but he will not be able to see them directly in his rearview mirror. Therefore, it is necessary for the officer to hold back several car lengths to allow the motorist room to observe and identify that an official emergency vehicle with active emergency lights is behind him. By watching traffic in a rearview mirror, one can notice that when a vehicle is fairly close the mirror will frame it from the roof to the bumper, and one can see how the lights would be cut off from view.

A siren may not always be necessary to effect a traffic stop. It is particularly desirable to avoid using a siren in heavy traffic, if possible. The use of a siren will often cause more confusion than understanding. People may not be sure of the direction from which the siren is coming and some may attempt to pull over to the right, while others may stop in traffic or slow down drastically, causing unnecessary problems.

There will be times when the siren will be necessary to emphasize the officer's authority and also to attract the attention of the driver of the vehicle which is the object of the officer's intentions. Often only a slight noise is necessary to attract the motorist's attention; usually, upon hearing a horn behind him, a person will look in his mirror, observe the emergency lights in operation, and will respond by pulling to the roadside. Some people believe that an officer cannot legally stop them without using the siren, and they will continue to drive, watching intently in the mirror, waiting for the siren. If a driver follows this procedure, it may be necessary to use the siren in order for him to comply. If a long distance is traveled or it is apparent that the violator is attempting to evade arrest, the siren becomes as much of a warning to other traffic of this hazard as an order for the violator to stop.

If an electrically powered, mechanical siren is used, it is important that it be sounded to its peak and then allowed to drop away to its lowest point. The purpose for this is to carry through all of the ranges of human hearing so that, hopefully, all persons within hearing distance of the siren will recognize it. Some people cannot hear very high notes and others do not respond well to low notes, which is why it is important to travel the full spectrum with an electro-mechanical siren in order to reach everyone. The electronic siren, which is in fact a tape recording amplified over a public address system, normally has a preset pattern of rise and fall which takes in this complete range. When using an electronic siren, the officer can turn it on and off, but he does not control its rise and fall. Some electronic siren consoles also have, in addition to the wailing sound, a "yelp," which is a rapid repetition of a very irritating sound frequency intended to attract attention with greater urgency than the normal siren sound. Some emergency vehicle operators use this "yelp" when traversing intersections in order to assure that all motorists are aware of their approach. Normally the use of a siren will be minimal in making a traffic stop in which the violator has observed and recognized the police vehicle behind him.

Many police vehicles are equipped with a public address system which enables the officer to speak to crowds and also to other motorists on the highway in order to communicate his orders. Sometimes during routine patrol, an officer will wish to notify a motorist of a very minor defect on his vehicle and will pull alongside, using his public address system to inform the motorist. It would be better to use the normal procedure for making a traffic stop and notify the person at the roadside than to confuse him by using the public address system. One can imagine the concern caused to a motorist who sees a police car alongside and hears an official voice coming from a public address system, obviously directed at him, but who cannot understand what is being said. His attention may just be attracted to the point that he will disregard his driving and become involved in a traffic accident.

When the officer believes that his public address system can be heard and understood, he needs to use language that is acceptable to all persons, avoid profanity, and keep his message brief. Sometimes it helps to speak to an identifiable description so that those who hear his words will know to whom he is speaking. For example, if the officer were addressing his remarks to a blue Ford™, which was the only blue Ford in this type of traffic, he might begin his comments by saying, "Driver of the blue Ford . . ." This will pinpoint the intent of the message. If the vehicle is from another state, he may use the name of that state as a means of address, e.g. "Oregon, your gas cap is missing," etc.

Public address systems can be very beneficial in controlling the movements of a driver and his passengers after a traffic stop has been made. If the officer wants the driver to exit from his vehicle and come back to him at the roadside, he may deliver that message efficiently by means of his public address system. It is important to use courtesy when speaking to people by means of a public address system. There is a sense of power which is received from being addressed by a loudspeaker. Therefore, it is not usually necessary for the officer to add any official emphasis or any rudeness in order to obtain compliance; the overpowering volume will do the job. It is just as easy and beneficial for the officer to temper his remarks with courtesy and friendliness. For example, the officer could say to a driver who has just pulled his vehicle to the roadside in response to emergency lights, "Sir, please get out of your car and come back here with me. Thank you." Saying "thank you" after making a request over a public address system is strongly suggestive that compliance is expected. These tactics are effective even with hostile motorists.

The officer can also control the movements of others in the vehicle by speaking to anyone who appears to be about to exit from the vehicle. He can say, "All other persons remain in the vehicle while I conduct my business with the driver. Thank you." It may be necessary to be more specific if this remark is ignored, e.g. addressing a specific person, "You in the blue sweater. Do not get out of the vehicle. My business is with the driver and for your own safety I want you to remain in the car. Thank you."

Public address systems are particularly effective for controlling pedestrians. If a pedestrian is walking down the road and the officer wishes to attract his attention, the public address system is one of the best ways to do so. It is also useful in speaking to a pedestrian who is violating the law. It not only attracts his attention but it draws the attention of other traffic to the violator. Sometimes this added peer pressure will embarrass the individual and have more effect upon future habits than will a traffic citation. Occasionally a daydreamer will walk against a pedestrian signal or red light or cross where crossing is not permitted, and an officer with a public address system can effectively admonish that pedestrian by saying, "Sir, the light is red, please return to the curb. Thank you." Or, "It is illegal to cross the street at this location. Please use the crosswalk for your own safety. Thank you."

A public address system is a one-way form of communication, thus limiting retort or argument. Since the public address system is loud and overbearing, it adds to the officer's aura of power and quite often guarantees compliance with his order.

The position of the patrol vehicle when making a traffic stop is essential to the safety of the officer and the violator. If the officer's vehicle is too close to that of the violator, the officer has very little room to operate or to withdraw from an attack. If it is too far away, there is obviously a gap in communication, and the officer has to go too far to reach his radio or the protection of his vehicle. Therefore, a distance of approximately two or three car lengths is recommended. This allows enough room to move about and yet keeps the situation confined to an adequate perimeter. If it is night, the patrol car headlights will better illuminate the vehicle and its interior.

Quite often the violator will be watching in his rearview mirror and responding to the movement of the patrol car when pulling to the roadside. As long as the officer keeps rolling, the violator will try to keep rolling. He's looking for a cue when to stop. Being aware of this, the officer can control the stop by ceasing his forward movement when both positions are in a safe location. The patrol car can be canted slightly to the left so that the officer has the additional protection of the left front fender added to his own door should he receive a hail of bullets upon stepping out of his car. In turning the vehicle slightly to the left, the right rear fender also becomes a point of cover for a backup officer who rolls up and needs to join the original officer in covering the stopped vehicle with an open field of fire.

Some officers believe that it is important to offset the patrol car slightly to the left so that the officer making a left-handed approach will be protected from traffic that might come too close and strike him while standing in the road. Since the practice of making a left-handed approach is discouraged in a later chapter as being an unsafe tactic, this is not encouraged as a position for the patrol car. Also, when an officer has had the opportunity to observe a stopped vehicle being struck by a moving vehicle, he will realize how little protection is really offered by the car sitting in that position. If speed is involved in the collision, the patrol car will also become a missile aimed in his direction rather than a barrier. It is recommended then that the patrol car be parked as far off the paved roadway as possible in order to avoid being struck by passing traffic.

All of the items discussed in this chapter are important at some time during a traffic stop. Making a traffic stop safely, completing the official business at hand, then resuming normal patrol requires more than a casual attitude. The guidelines offered in this chapter are based on the career experience of the author and others who have developed through the years the safe practice of making traffic stops as part of their routine work. It may appear to the untrained observer that the officer following these guidelines is relaxed and casual (both desirable), but it is an illusion to think that he is not alert and aware. The use of his equipment and of his mind in controlling the situation surrounding a roadside traffic stop will prevent injury and property damage in most situations.

CHAPTER FOUR

ENFORCEMENT TACTICS AND SAFETY DURING TRAFFIC STOPS

THE MATERIAL in this chapter is intended to provide the reader with the necessary knowledge to accomplish the following:
- Recognize the hazards inherent in a "routine" traffic stop
- Develop tactics for accomplishing a safe traffic stop
- Increase total sensory awareness of danger signs during a roadside enforcement contact
- Develop teamwork with a partner
- Position the patrol vehicle for maximum protection to the officer

The "routine stop" has probably killed or injured more traffic officers in the line of duty than anything else. The "routine" nature of the stop is in the mind of the officer. When one is engaged in a continuous activity, such as stopping vehicles for traffic violations, the activity becomes routine. Unfortunately, the hazard of a driver who is also a fleeing felon or who is psychotic could be found in the next stop. Too often the officer who is specializing in traffic enforcement begins to think almost exclusively in terms of traffic violations. When he stops a vehicle for exceeding the speed limit, his mind may very well be occupied with only that violation. If he has not encountered a hostile driver or some more physical form of resistance in the near past, he will very likely be complaisant when he makes the approach. He may anticipate resentment in verbal form, but statistics show he just may encounter a "fatal dose" of resentment.

Enforcement Tactics and Safety During Traffic Stops 37

Numerous examples can be cited on this subject. One incident involved a California Highway Patrol officer who had stopped a vehicle for speed on a freeway. The vehicle contained two occupants, both male. The officer was in the process of issuing a citation to the driver when his outside radio speaker began to broadcast a "wanted" bulletin for two suspects wanted in an armed robbery which had recently occurred in a nearby city. Both occupants of the stopped vehicle got out and walked back to the officer, obviously intent upon the information contained in the broadcast. The officer thought this was unusual, but he continued to write the citation. The description of the wanted vehicle and suspects was entirely different from the vehicle and the two men which the officer had stopped. He completed the citation, and the vehicle and occupants continued on their way. Within three minutes, a second broadcast was received by the officer reporting another armed robbery which had occurred in another nearby city, and this one matched the vehicle and the two men whom he had just stopped! The officer gave chase, and with the assistance of other units was able to overtake and capture the suspects without further incident. It was very fortunate for him that the broadcasts came in the order that they did. The suspects later told detectives that if they had heard their own descriptions on the officer's outside speaker they would have killed him on the spot. As long as he was issuing a traffic citation and apparently unaware of their identity, they chose not to add murder to their other crimes.

Another example which further illustrates the point of this discussion is one from the author's own experience. While working as a traffic officer for a city police department, I observed a vehicle go through a red signal at a busy intersection. Upon stopping the vehicle, I noted that there was a total of six male adults occupying the front and back seats of the sedan. It was a warm summer day, and I was feeling relaxed and even lazy. I approached the driver's window and advised him of the violation and my intention to cite him. I looked into the interior of the vehicle at the other occupants. They were young and had the look of trouble, yet they all sat very quietly and said nothing. I did notice that one subject in the back seat nearest to me was wearing a coat. I thought that this was unusual because of the heat of the day, but I did not dwell on it. The thought crossed my mind that if I were to examine the identification of each subject and run them all through the dispatcher, I would probably come up with one who was wanted. Instead, I allowed the laziness of the warm summer afternoon to prevail, issued the citation, and returned to my patrol car. Two days later, I was summoned to the detective bureau of the police department, and when I entered the office of the detective, I saw that on his desk was a copy of my citation. He asked if I recalled issuing it and I replied that I did. He then asked me if I recalled anyone in the vehicle wearing a coat. I did remember the man sitting nearest to me in the back seat and I replied in the affirmative. The detective laid a mug shot next to the citation. The mug had been taken in San Quentin Prison, and it was a photograph of the man wearing the coat. He advised me that this man was an escapee from San Quentin Prison and that he was now in custody as a result of an informant's tip-off. When he was captured, it was found that he was in possession of a loaded .45 automatic pistol. He had been carrying the pistol under the coat on the day of the traffic stop and had stated to the other occupants of the vehicle when I stopped them, "If this pig starts checking IDs, I'm going to waste him." Apparently, my laziness saved my life in this case.

Is it possible for a traffic officer to approach an unknown vehicle and its occupants on the roadside without exposing himself unnecessarily to hostile fire or other attack? The answer is *yes*. The problem is that most police officers approach vehicles in entirely the wrong manner and place themselves totally at the mercy of those who occupy the vehicle. This may be the reason why traffic stops rate very high on the scale of events in which police officers are killed in the line of duty. Most of the time, in analyzing the situation, it is very apparent that the officer was careless in some way and placed himself in jeopardy. I have personally heard inmates of the jail say that when they were stopped and arrested, it was their intention to kill the officer but "he never gave me a chance." Such testimony to an officer's diligence is worthy of consideration. If the officer were alert and aware and projected this to the suspect at all times during the transaction at the roadside, I believe that fewer deaths or injuries would occur as the result of assault. However, diligence and alertness alone will not always suffice to keep an officer alive. There are some situations so deadly in premeditation that more is required in the way of safety practices.

One of the other constant hazards to a traffic officer while making an enforcement stop is traffic itself. If the officer is making the usual routine approach from the driver's side, he will find himself standing in the roadway at the edge of the traffic lane. Depending on the volume of the traffic, this may be a very hazardous location. Cars and trucks passing by within inches can be very distracting, and the officer must split his attention between the traffic and the errant motorist.

If there are other occupants in the vehicle, this is another point of concentration for the officer. Added to his need for awareness of his radio via the outside speaker, the officer's attention is divided four ways. Any number of things can occur in this situation. The officer may be "picked off" by a passing car driven by an intoxicated or careless driver. If he stands directly in front of the driver's door while talking with the driver through the window, he is in direct line with the door when it opens. If the driver suddenly decides to get out of his car or open his door suddenly for any other reason, it may very well knock the officer backward into the traffic lane. If the timing of that act coincides with the passing of a large truck, a traffic officer has been lost. If the officer stands forward of the driver's car so that he may look into the interior of the car and also face to the rear and observe approaching traffic, he is essentially cut off from his patrol car by the opening of the driver's door. If the driver does open his door and hold it in an open position, the officer now must either go out into the traffic lane or completely around the violator's vehicle to reach his own car and his radio.

While standing at the driver's door, the officer is a perfect target for small arms fire within the vehicle. If the driver or one of the occupants is armed with a firearm and does have the intention to shoot the officer, there is very little the officer can do to avoid it in that position. Presuming that he is in the "routine stop" state of mind, he will probably not anticipate the possibility of a weapon until he sees it. When he does see it, he may have less than a second to react. These possibilities are not in his favor at that time. He is totally without cover. The driver of the vehicle can easily shoot him no matter where he is standing in relation to the door. Some officers make it a practice to stand just back of the trailing edge of the driver's door, causing the driver to turn in an awkward position to look back at them, which they believe gives them some margin of safety; unfortunately, it does not. If the driver is holding a hand gun at waist level out of sight, he has but to open the door a few inches and discharge the weapon into the officer's midsection. The driver could even raise the weapon to the windowsill level and fire before the officer could react. If the officer does react, the odds are against him. If he chooses to run away, he is a good target for quite a distance before he gets to cover. If he chooses to draw his own weapon in an attempt to fire on the suspect first, unless he is the reincarnation of his early American cousin, the frontier marshal, he will probably lose the contest. The reason for this discussion is to point out the hoplessness of the officer's position when making a traffic stop approach on the driver's side of the vehicle.

What, then, are the alternatives? There are several. The first suggestion is that the officer's attention be riveted upon the vehicle and its occupants from the moment he turns on his emergency lights to signal the driver to stop. He needs to be aware of the number of occupants that are visible. It is possible that there are some who are not visible at the time of the stop. One of the most heart-stopping moments I have had as a traffic officer was when I was standing at the driver's door, receiving the driver's license and talking to a person whom I thought was the only occupant of the vehicle. While I was in conversation with the driver, a person who had been asleep in the back seat sat up abruptly to my immediate right. The sudden appearance of his head, when I had thought no one was there, caused me considerable alarm. He could just as well have been lying there on purpose, rather than asleep, and risen for the purpose of shooting me. With this in mind, an officer needs to approach a vehicle slowly and with a great deal of awareness. His awareness of the vehicle need not be limited to sight and hearing. The sense of touch can also be added. The more senses that are working for him, the more likely it is that he will be successful. Upon approaching the vehicle at arm's length, the officer should place his hand on the fender and pause just long enough to feel for movement within the vehicle. If he sees only one or two occupants who are sitting very still and yet feels movement within the vehicle, it is a sign that there is something or someone else unseen. He should withdraw to the safety of his patrol car and consider calling for a backup unit. The movement he felt may be the result of someone lying down in the back seat. It could even be a kidnap victim in the trunk squirming around trying to attract attention, or an animal being transported in the trunk. The movement could be harmless, but until that is proven it should be treated as a danger signal.

One way in which the officer can make contact with the driver of the other car without exposing himself as previously described is to gesture for the driver to get out of his car. This can be done by making eye contact by means of the driver's rearview mirror and motioning for him to get out of the car. When he opens his door, verbal directions can be added. This should be done from the safety of the patrol car door. Ballistics tests have shown that a car door with the window down will deflect most small arms ammunition, due to the angle of the door and its construction. Therefore, the officer has a fairly good shield in his car door which he may use while directing the driver out of his vehicle. In order not to be in the line of traffic which is passing on the roadway, the officer should pull his patrol car as far to the right as he can.

Upon the approach of the driver, the officer should direct him to a place near the right front fender of the patrol car. This is a location of safety for the violator, and it is also to the officer's advantage to have him there. This advantage is based on the proximity to the patrol car and its equipment. If the officer is standing near the right front fender of the patrol car facing the violator and his car, he has a clear field of view of almost everything that may be a hazard to him. If he is at least one car width from the traffic lane, he is fairly safe and can visually ignore the flow of traffic from the rear during the stop. It is a good idea, however, for the officer to keep listening for the sound of approaching vehicles, especially if the sound of screeching tires is heard. If the officer needs to use his radio during the roadside transaction, he is very close to the right front door and may easily reach inside the door and obtain the communications he needs, yet maintain control of the situation and the violator. In the event of hostile gunfire from the suspect vehicle, the officer has access to cover in the form of the right front door of the patrol car as well as communication for summoning help through his radio and the additional fire power of his shotgun.

None of these will be available if the right front door of the patrol car is locked. Many officers drive their entire shift with the right front door locked, if they are riding alone; this is a dangerous thing to do. Access to the interior of the patrol vehicle from the right may be necessary at any time during the shift, and quite often the keys are hanging in the ignition while the officer is outside of the vehicle. This means that the only access can be obtained by going completely around the car and entering from the street side. If the officer were under attack, he might not make it.

Another way to make contact with the driver is through right side approach. This is done by exiting the patrol car after both vehicles have stopped and going quickly between the cars to a point near the right rear fender of the violator's vehicle. At that time, it is important that the officer be aware of who and what is in the suspect vehicle. The officer's awareness can be increased by adding the sense of touch to his information. If he will place his hand on the trunk or fender of the violator's vehicle and briefly feel for movement, he will know more than if he uses only his eyes and ears. Should he feel movement in the vehicle, but the persons visible to him are not moving, then it is apparent that someone else is present whom he cannot see. It would be prudent at that time to withdraw to his vehicle and summon a backup unit. If he pauses at that point and feels no movement, then it is time to proceed to the nearest window at that side and look in. The contents of the vehicle and all occupants should be observed carefully in order to be aware of everything that is occurring. When the officer is in a position to see the front seat area of the violator's vehicle, he is ready to deal with the driver. If the driver is alone it is possible, by either opening the right front door or having the window lowered, to transact most of the business from this position. It may be advisable, if it is a low vehicle and uncomfortable to stand near, for the officer to direct the driver out of the car and back to a point near his vehicle. If there are other passengers in the vehicle over whom the officer must reach in order to transact his business with the driver, it is recommended that the driver be removed from the vehicle. This will eliminate (or at least reduce) the probability that passengers will interfere with the officer's business with the driver; it is also safer. If the driver is alone in the vehicle, the officer now has an improved view of the interior. He can see both the front and back seats as well as anything that is lying on the front seat. If he were standing on the driver's side of the car, his view of the front seat would be limited by the driver's body, the pillar post of the windshield, etc., but from the right side he has a clear view. Another advantage of this position is his view of the glove compartment; the officer has a direct view of its interior. If there is a weapon inside, his chances of seeing it are good. Yet another advantage to the right side approach is the fact that the officer now has cover and concealment in the event of hostile gunfire from within the vehicle. When he was on the left side of the car, he was at the driver's mercy because the driver could lean out of the window and see the officer at any point. On the right side of the vehicle, this is not the case. As soon as the officer sees a hostile movement, which involves a gunbarrel being pointed in his direction, he can drop to the ground. As soon as his head clears the windowsill of the vehicle, he is protected from gunfire. It is not recommended that he stay in that position very long. The driver will probably slide over to get a better shot. By that time the officer should be back to his patrol car and calling for assistance from behind the safety of the right front door.

There is no 100 percent safe way to deal with criminal behavior in human beings at the roadside. It is possible to do things more safely than is being done at present by many officers. Using the right side approach and bringing the driver back to the right front fender of the patrol car are both ways to improve the officer's safety and advantage over the violator.

When two officers are working as a team, it is important that they function as a team. If a traffic stop is made, it should be decided that one officer will make the approach while the other remains behind the safety of his door. This is an insurance policy against surprises. It may be well to make sure that the driver knows that there are two officers in this vehicle. This can be accomplished by brief conversation between the officers during the stop. When the driver knows that there is a second officer, it does limit the probability that he will attempt an assault. It is also beneficial for the second officer to remain behind the cover of his door. This will add to the suspect's apprehension about firing on the officer who is not protected. Should anything go wrong and the approaching officer becomes a hostage, the second officer must remain steadfast in his position of safety while awaiting further assistance. He will have the benefit of the radio and the accessibility of the shotgun. He is covered from the suspect's gunfire and, unless he foolishly gives up his weapon, he holds the winning cards. It is possible that a psychotic suspect may shoot the officer who has made the approach. However, if he does this, he has lost any bargaining power that he may have had and will probably be immediately fired upon by the second officer. Therefore, it contributes to stalling tactics for the second officer to remain behind cover and accessible to his communications equipment. Time is on his side.

Also important to the officer's safety is the way in which he stands when facing a violator on the street. For a person to stand flat footed and face an opponent front to front is to share the tendency to fall down. A shove to the chest or a jerking forward of the uniform fabric will cause the officer to fall, since he has nothing to brace him front or rear. However, if the officer will make a one-half right turn so that his left foot is pointing at the center of the suspect's body and his right foot is back 18 to 20 inches and pointing to the side, he will have formed a strong base with leverage front and rear. This will allow him to resist a push or pull and also execute a push or pull from his standpoint. By turning a half turn to the right, he will have removed his weapon from direct access to the suspect, making it just a little more difficult for the suspect to remove the weapon from the holster. When the officer is standing in this position with his knees slightly flexed and his weight primarily on the balls of his feet, he is in a ready position of advantage. The position may be altered if the officer is left handed so that everything is reversed, but the results will be the same. The officer should always stand with his weapon away from the suspect in this slightly half-right position of advantage.

When writing a citation at the right front fender of the patrol car, it will be tempting sometimes to use the fender as a desk. Some officers consistently write citations in this manner, leaning forward on their patrol car hood and writing the citation, leaving themselves exposed to attack from the suspect. When turning in this manner and facing the patrol car, a right-handed officer is practically offering his weapon for the suspect's taking. Instead, the officer should remain erect in the position of advantage described previously and hold the citation book in his hands at chest level for the writing of the citation. This will take some practice to become comfortable, but once the habit is established, the officer will be safer. If the suspect strikes out and reaches for the officer, it is probable that the officer will catch the movement and be able to drop his citation book and bring his hands upward to deflect the blow. By having the hands already up front during the writing of the citation, they are available for other, more important things such as self-defense. It is better for the officer to drop the citation book and scatter its contents than to be the recipient of an attack from which he cannot defend himself because he was not in a position to do so.

These techniques are not original to this author, nor are they unique. They are, however, much safer than the other methods presently used by many officers. It is recommended that these suggestions be practiced by setting up simulated traffic stops and walking through the procedure until it is comfortable. Once it is comfortable, the officer should continue to practice until the right way is more comfortable than the wrong way.

CHAPTER FIVE

HANDLING VIOLATORS DURING A TRAFFIC STOP

THE MATERIAL in this chapter is intended to provide the reader with the necessary information to accomplish the following:

* Develop a style of approach which will not degrade the violator
* Develop tactics which will avoid confrontation during a traffic stop
* Develop an understanding of what emotions are motivating certain violators by their behavior
* Utilize some basic concepts of psychology to remain in control of the situation

It is important that the officer recognize the necessity of maintaining a courteous and equal relationship with a traffic violator. When the officer assumes an overbearing or morally superior attitude toward the person he has stopped, he is unconsciously setting up a confrontation. No one likes to be told he is wrong, especially an adult. The officer's patrol car and his uniform will set him apart well enough as a symbol of authority without the necessity of overbearing behavior on his part.

Upon approaching a violator who has been stopped, one of the first things I always do is greet the person with a smile and a friendly tone of voice. The greeting is completely removed from the business of the traffic violation. I may start out by saying, "Good morning, how are you today," and saying it in a convincing, sincere manner. It is so startling to the citizen to have this type of greeting begin the usually unpleasant transaction at the roadside that many of them are at a loss for words. Some even ask to have the greeting repeated by saying, "What did you say?" The advantage is immediately in the hands of the officer when he does the unexpected. Unfortunately, the general public expects the officer to be overbearing and officious. When he behaves differently it is confusing. This confusion will quite often give way to pleasant surprise.

When the officer has made his initial contact and has completed his friendly greeting, it is time to deal with the issue of the traffic violation. It is the common practice of some traffic officers to immediately demand to see the driver's license. Persons expecting this demand will often have their driver's licenses ready. Sometimes I think that becoming preoccupied with the driver's license gives the officer some thinking time that he needs in order to deal with his own nervousness. Most officers do not realize that they too are nervous, but it is a fact. The motorist may ask the question, "What did I do wrong?" Even though the driver is aware of his violation, he wants to be reassured that he is correct and that the officer has not spotted something else.

The issue of the driver's license can become a point of contention if improperly handled. The officer's immediate demand of the driver's license could be met by the driver's question, "What did I do wrong?" The officer's reply might be, "Give me your driver's license and I will tell you." What will he do when confronted with a rebellious driver who says, "You tell me what I did, and I'll give you my driver's license"? Confrontation is not necessary; the driver's license can wait.

The officer's friendly approach initially described in this chapter should carry throughout the contact. After having greeted the motorist, he may then deal with the issue of the violation by saying, in a friendly manner, "Did you realize that you were going 10 miles an hour over the speed limit?" When placed in the context of a possible oversight on his part, the violation does not seem as serious and the driver may feel that he is able to save some face. This is not intended to belittle or diminish the importance of safe driving and obeying the laws. It is only a matter of presentation technique. Later, in this discussion with the driver, the officer may generally emphasize the importance of safe driving without ramming it down the violator's throat.

If the driver has passengers in the vehicle, further problems may be eliminated by asking him to exit from his vehicle and meet the officer at the roadside. When this is done, the loss of privacy is avoided. The conversation between the officer and the violator, while standing out in the open air and away from the hearing of passengers, leaves the matter in the hands of the motorist to tell his passengers whatever he wishes about the contact. The necessity for him to stand up to the officer in order to look masculine or tough is also removed. People usually behave differently when they are alone than when in the company of friends or loved ones.

When a male driver is stopped and has his family, his wife, or his girlfriend with him, the officer can spare the driver's male ego of having the woman watch while he is lectured on a driving violation, or of thinking that his children are seeing him as a lesser man because of the officer's position of authority. Removing the driver from the presence of these people will be a much appreciated favor and may very well prevent verbal or physical resistance in the process.

The officer will have better success if he avoids becoming the finger-shaking parent or teacher when dealing with traffic violators. It will be difficult to avoid this role when so many errant "children" are seen behind the wheels of automobiles driving recklessly and carelessly. However, no adult likes to be lectured in such a manner, and it will bring about a confrontation more quickly than a friendly, nonaccusatory approach. People are responsible for their actions, and when the officer documents his observation of a traffic offense and binds the driver over to the court, he is furthering that responsibility in a legal way. It is not necessary to berate the individual after having notified him of the reason for the stop and beginning the issuance of a citation. It is desirable to continue conversing with the person in a light manner in order to pass the time while the citation is being completed. Usually, subjects other than the traffic violation are safer to pursue. On several occasions people have said to me, "It sure is hard to be mad at you when you are being so nice." By not assuming the role of an ogre, the officer is diminishing the tendency of the violator to react in a negative manner.

It is possible for the officer to be alert and watchful for signs of aggression and to protect himself from harm without assuming a paranoid posture. He can be friendly and not demeaning in his conduct and still accomplish his task. People will appreciate being treated as equals and not as naughty children.

Quite often personal problems such as marital conflict, emotional disturbances, illness, etc., will cause people not to concentrate on their driving habits. If they are very upset it is unlikely that being stopped by a policeman will improve their frame of mind. Sometimes people become very angry with themselves for having done something to cause them to be stopped by an officer. The anger that they feel for themselves is all too often projected toward the officer. It may even develop into the use of profanity and the directing of personal insults at the officer. Considerable self-restraint will be required to avoid responding in kind to this type of verbal attack. It is important to realize that the officer is in charge of the situation and has nothing personally to lose during the contact. On the other hand, the violator is probably embarrassed and may be concerned about having to pay a fine. Sometimes these emotions can be pointed out by saying, "Sir, I realize that you are angry with yourself for your carelessness, but the way you are behaving now can be dangerous to your health. If you keep working yourself up like this, you may have a heart attack. Why don't you relax while I write this citation." Here the officer is pointing out to the person that he is really angry with his own actions. In some cases the person will recognize this and even apologize for his remarks. If he does not recognize it immediately, the seed may have been planted for a later realization. In any event, the officer needs to avoid taking personally any comments of a derogatory nature that he hears while performing his duties. If some drivers, particularly males, are contacted in the presence of their friends, the officer may have the opportunity to see such behavior more frequently. In some cases, it is even predictable.

It was stated earlier that the officer needs to avoid the role of a finger-shaking parent. Being a police officer is definitely a parentlike role, and the violator very easily slips into the role of a naughty child. Since that is an uncomfortable role for an adult, it will probably generate hostile feelings. If the officer will say to himself, on occasion, "This person is my equal, this person is an adult, I want to treat him with respect as I would be treated," it will definitely help to control the attitude which he projects.

It takes two to make an argument. If the officer does not allow the relationship to generate into a person-to-person confrontation, he will be better off. Recognizing that the violator probably sees him in the role of a parent figure will help the officer to avoid playing that part.

Sir Robert Peel, who founded the British Police System in 1829, has espoused nine principles for police officers to follow in their duties. One of the principles directly relates to the officer-violator contact in a traffic stop. Remembering its content may very well help the officer in remaining on equal footing with the citizen behind the wheel. The principle states as follows: "The police at all times should maintain a relationship with the public that gives reality to the historic tradition that the police are the public and that the public are the police: the police are the only members of the public who are paid to give fulltime attention to duties which are encumbent on every citizen in the interest of community welfare."

The above principle reemphasizes the equality of the violator and the officer. It also establishes the need for the officer's presence on the highway and the further need for his actions in stopping careless motorists to prevent traffic accidents.

CHAPTER SIX

EXAMINING IDENTIFICATION DOCUMENTS

THE MATERIAL in this chapter is intended to provide the reader with the necessary information to accomplish the following:

- Evaluate the information on the face of personal identification documents
- Recognize discrepancies in personal identification documents
- Evaluate the information on the face of vehicle registration documents
- Recognize discrepancies in vehicle registration documents.

Receiving and examining documents of identification are routine parts of the traffic officer's work. The most common document encountered will be the driver's license. It is a fairly simple and fairly short form, but quite often it is not read or fully understood by the officer. The driver's license may become a prop in the hand of the officer to look at and gesture with while talking to a motorist at the roadside. It is important that this does not occur. The driver's license is one of the most abused forms of identification in terms of fraud and counterfeiting. It also is quite often altered if the face of the document is not encased in plastic or some other material which would prevent access to the paper surface. Some states in the United States use plastic stock for their driver's licenses, and the letters and numerals are raised from the surface as with a credit card. These are obviously more difficult to alter.

Examining Identification Documents

One of the first points to look at on a driver's license or other identification document is the photograph of the person to whom it belongs. If the document contains the photograph, it should be immediately compared with the person who has presented it. There will be some changes in a person's appearance over a period of years, such as the length of hair, color of hair, the addition or removal of a beard or mustache, etc. If the photograph does not routinely match the bearer, an inquiry should be made as to the reason. A scan of the printed material on the face of the driver's license needs to be done with some thought. For instance, if the officer is not registering in his mind what he is seeing, he may well overlook an expiration date, which has passed, or a change of address. One of the quickest ways to verify the address is to ask the presenter the question, "What is your present address?" Sometimes the person will answer by saying, "It's the same as on this license." This may possibly be an effort to evade giving valid information. If this occurs, the officer should insist that the person repeat the street address where he lives at the present time.

The traffic officer can discipline his mind to do two things at once. He can read the driver's license and interpret the data while observing the subject and maintaining a safe posture. The physical description on the driver's license can be quickly compared with that of the person who stands before him. If discrepancies are noted in height or weight, hair coloring, or eye coloring, they need to be investigated. Any evidence of tampering with the face data of a driver's license also needs to be investigated. The date of birth may be one area of alteration when dealing with a very young person. The driver's license, which is very easily acquired, is a favorite source of identification and is accepted by many as proof of age. A young person who wishes to be served alcoholic beverages may alter the birthdate in order to appear older. This cannot usually be done without showing some evidence of tampering.

A driver's license is one of the easiest forms of identification to acquire. Usually a Department of Motor Vehicle (DMV) will not pursue proof of identity beyond a cursory questioning of the applicant. Sometimes additional identification is required, but not in all cases. The officer can verify the information on the driver's license by requesting additional identification. If all identity documents presented are new appearing, he needs to be suspicious. Most people have identification that is issued at various times in their lives and will show various signs of age. If all documents appear to be new, it may be that this person has recently acquired a new identity.

A new traffic officer can sharpen his ability to evaluate the face data on a driver's license by studying his own driver's license and becoming thoroughly familiar with the items found thereon. If he becomes comfortable with looking at various parts of the license for certain information, he will not easily pass over these areas when examining a license at the roadside.

There are still some states and foreign countries which issue driver's licenses and identification documents that are not laminated and that do not contain a photograph. These are obviously natural targets for the forger. If the license is issued in a foreign jurisdiction, it is not quite as easy for the officer to verify the information. If no photograph is attached, and if the material on the face of the document is typed, it could be just as well fraudulent as valid. This type of document should automatically stimulate the officer to require additional identification.

Another document which is a routine part of a traffic stop is the vehicle registration. Too often this document is accepted by merely noting the name of the registered owner to be the same as that on the driver's license. It is important that the officer verify further. This can be done by knowing that the license number of the plates attached to the vehicle is also a part of the registration document. The vehicle identification number (VIN) is the best source of verification for an automobile. If the VIN and the license plate number both match the registration document, then the probability is good that the vehicle is in the hands of its proper owner.

One vehicle theft technique that is popular in the United States is the salvage switch. This is accomplished by purchasing a wrecked vehicle from a salvage yard along with registration and title. The purchaser expresses the intent to restore the vehicle. He then takes the title, registration, and license plates from the wreckage, finds a vehicle which generally matches in year and model, steals it, and attaches the license plates from the wreck. If he is stopped by a policeman, the registration will match the license plates and also will be in the name of the driver. A quick glance at the registration will indicate that all is well. If the officer were to pursue his investigation further by matching the VIN with the registration document, he would find a discrepancy. This would be sufficient cause to hold the vehicle and driver for further investigation.

Registration documents and titles are often counterfeited. The counterfeiter's press can more easily produce blanks matching the design of a state's title of ownership than counterfeit money. One ownership document would be worth thousands of of dollars if matched up with a stolen vehicle.

Registration and title can easily be obtained by mail from some jurisdictions when accompanied by a check for the amount of the registration fee. Since this is done by mail, the issuing agency never sees the vehicle. Therefore, it would be easy to apply for a nonexistent vehicle, or one which the applicant intended to steal.

There are enough ways to falsify paperwork that an officer needs to be very skeptical when examining documents. The vehicle registration and title documents are very common instruments of theft, and it is important that the traffic officer scrutinize each one. He also has the resources of the Department of Motor Vehicle's files at his disposal as well as other computerized information which will assist him in determining validity. This will not be accomplished unless the officer pursues each document that he encounters with the same diligence. He should be suspicious and thorough.

CHAPTER SEVEN

AUTOMOTIVE EQUIPMENT INSPECTION

THE MATERIAL in this chapter is intended to provide the reader with the necessary information to accomplish the following:

- Inspect the basic safety equipment of an automobile at the roadside in less than five minutes
- Inspect the safety equipment of a truck at the roadside
- Develop the knowledge necessary to recognize defects in vehicle safety equipment
- Develop techniques that will detect equipment defects on vehicles observed while on patrol

Familiarity with the basic safety equipment of automobiles and trucks is important for the traffic officer. He need not be an accomplished mechanic, but it is necessary that he understand the basic workings of automotive equipment. During a roadside stop for any reason, it is possible to conduct a quick inspection of the vehicle's safety equipment and possibly avoid a traffic accident by detecting a dangerous defect.

The equipment of an automobile is relatively easy to inspect and can be done in a short time, probably in less than five minutes. When an officer has the occasion to inspect the equipment of an automobile, he needs to follow a specific procedure which will include the safety items.

Some of the inspection of an automobile's safety equipment can be accomplished visually when observing the vehicle in traffic and also upon approaching the vehicle during a traffic stop.

For instance, the officer will be able to see if the safety glass on the vehicle is intact in all windows and whether or not it is free of defects. Defects would include cracks or broken areas that obstruct the driver's view. While contacting the driver of the vehicle, the officer should be able to see the windshield wipers and tell whether the blades are defective. Another easily visible item is the condition of the tires.

When conducting a specific inspection of an automobile's safety equipment, the officer should have the driver manipulate the items under his control at the officer's direction so that he may verify their condition. This can be done quickly and without unnecessary delay for the driver. It is important that the officer stress the safety aspect of this inspection in order to solicit the driver's cooperation and understanding.

While inspecting the automobile during the daytime, the following items should receive specific attention.

Windshield wipers. If the blades appear to be in good condition, the officer can ask the driver to operate the motor to determine that the blades move smoothly across the glass.

Horn. The horn should be sounded to determine that it does work and that it emits an audible sound which can be heard in normal traffic. The horn is a warning device and is a very important item since it may avoid a traffic collision.

Turn signals. The turn signals should be checked front and rear, not only to determine if they are functioning, but also to take note of the rate of flash. If the flashing cycle is excessively rapid, they may not be clearly visible. If the signals flash more than 100 times a minute, this can be considered excessively fast and should be repaired. Adversely, if the flash cycle is very slow so that it might be missed due to the delay between flashes, it is equally important that repair be initiated. Any flash rate below 60 flashes per minute is too slow.

Brake lights. The brake lights can be tested by having the driver apply the brake pedal several times and observe whether the lights are functioning. It is useful to examine the brake lights while the taillights are also engaged. If the taillights are on, the driver cannot manipulate the light switch in order to simulate brake lights. The taillights should remain lighted while the brake lights go on and off when the pedal is depressed.

Lamp lenses. The condition of the lenses for all lamps on the exterior of the vehicle should be inspected. If there are cracks or pieces broken out of the lenses, they should be repaired.

Hydraulic brake system. The brake pedal is one of the only ways the officer has of inspecting the hydraulic brake system on an automobile while the vehicle is standing still. The officer should have the driver depress the brake pedal and observe its travel. If the vehicle is equipped with power brakes it will be difficult to determine the condition of the brakes by observing the pedal alone. However, if the brake pedal goes immediately to the floorboard upon the first application, this is a clear indication that the brakes are defective. While checking tires is a good time to look for brake fluid leaking down the inside of the wheels.

Parking brake. The parking brake can be tested by having the driver set it tightly and then put the vehicle in gear at the idle. If the brake holds the vehicle back, without slipping, the brake will proably hold on most hills. On a vehicle with an automatic transmission this test at the idle with the vehicle in drive will provide a sufficient test. On a vehicle which has a manual transmission, the officer should have the driver engage second gear and release the clutch slowly. If the engine stalls as the clutch is engaged, it is a good indication that the vehicle has an inadequate parking brake.

While observing the manipulation of these controls, the officer can also have the driver turn the steering wheel and observe the amount of play that exists. If the vehicle is equipped with power steering, the driver should be able to turn the steering wheel effortlessly with one hand while the officer observes an immediate reaction in the front wheels. A vehicle not equipped with power steering can be inspected by observing the amount of travel in the steering wheel before any effect is observed in the front tires. If the steering wheel goes a quarter of a turn or more before tightening up, this is an indication of excessive play in the steering.

Tires. The condition of the tires can be visually observed by walking around the vehicle and looking at the tread depth. A simple test of sufficient tread depth is to insert the edge of a penny into the tread groove. If the edge of the groove does not come to Lincoln's head then the depth is insufficient for safety. The amount of tire tread required by law will vary from one jurisdiction to another. The purpose of grooves in a tire is to allow water to escape when driving on wet roads. If the water cannot escape, there will be a tendency for the tire to climb up onto the surface of the water and hydroplane, which takes the vehicle out of the driver's control.

An item which does not come under the category of safety, but definitely one toward which the officer needs to direct his attention is the muffler system. If the engine noise is noticeably loud, it may be an indication that the muffler is defective. It may also be an indication that the muffler system has been modified to amplify the vehicle's noise. This also is illegal in many states. The one safety aspect of a muffler system is that it carries the exhaust gases from the engine to a point of escape away from the vehicle. If the muffler system is defective, carbon monoxide gas may be leaking into the passenger's compartment of the vehicle and can cause sleepiness and illness on the part of the occupants. Many deaths are caused every year by carbon monoxide poisoning. It is not always possible to detect the presence of carbon monoxide in the passenger compartment, but if the driver is exposed to it, it may cause him to go to sleep at the wheel and result in a fatal accident.

If the lights of the vehicle are inspected at night, it is important to observe both the high and low beams of the headlights. A guide to follow for general safety is to measure visually whether the low beam extends to a point at least 100 feet ahead of the vehicle and the high beam at least 350 feet ahead. These distances should be consistent under all loading conditions. Headlamp adjustment cannot be precisely determined by observing where the beam strikes the roadway. However, if the lamps are out of adjustment, usually it will be noticeable, especially when the beams are uneven.

It is not expected that the average traffic officer will be expert enough to thoroughly inspect the brake system on a truck. It is possible for a non-truck driver to learn how to inspect an air brake system at the roadside to determine certain obvious defects. The following are some of the items to look for when checking a truck's brake system. Most of the items can be determined while the officer is standing on the running board of the cab and having the driver follow his instructions.

Single control. There should be a single control to operate the brakes on the tractor as well as the trailers, in combination. This can be determined by having the driver apply the foot brake and listening and observing for a reaction from the brakes on the trailer(s).

Pressure gauge. A clearly visible pressure gauge should be mounted in the cab so that the driver can monitor the air pressure in the brake system. This gauge should be monitored by the officer while conducting the roadside test of the air brake system.

Warning device. The truck should be equipped with a warning device which may be either audible, visual, or both. The audible warning is normally in the form of a buzzer that sounds when the air pressure drops below the safe level, and the visual is usually a flag that drops down within the driver's view to indicate low air pressure.

While conducting a roadside brake test on a truck, the officer can have the driver continuously apply his foot pedal and observe the drop in air pressure that occurs on the pressure gauge. As the air pressure drops to a range between a maximum 75 pounds per square inch (PSI) and 55 PSI, the warning device should activate. If it does not, this is an indication of a defect. Without a warning device during this range, a truck driver may lose sufficient air pressure to stop his vehicle in an emergency.

Emergency stopping system. While requiring the driver to manipulate the brake pedal and observing the drop in air pressure on the pressure gauge, the officer should have him continue until the air pressure reaches a range between 45 PSI and 20 PSI. Somewhere during that range the emergency stopping system on the truck and trailers should activate. This means that when the low pressure range is reached, the brake system automatically activates, bringing the vehicle to a halt while there is still sufficient air.

The emergency stopping system has a release lever in the cab, and when the automatic system has been activated, the driver should be able to release it from his seat. The officer should ask him to do so to determine if this control is working. Another way to verify the emergency stopping system is to ask the driver to dismount from the cab and have him break the connection by opening the glad hands between the tractor and the trailer. Upon this breaking of the line, the emergency stopping system should activate immediately and hold the brakes for at least fifteen minutes. When these procedures have been completed, the officer should have the driver increase the RPM of the engine to observe the pressure increase on the pressure gauge. If the system is in good condition, it should not take very long for the pressure to build up again to a normal range above 100 PSI.

Another test of the general condition of an air brake system is to instruct the driver to release the petcock on the wet air tank. There are two tanks, wet and dry, located underneath the tractor and each trailer. The wet tank captures pollutants in the system, which are oil and water. It should be a safety practice to drain the wet tank on a daily basis in order to avoid a collection of pollutants. The officer should have the driver open the petcock slowly, allowing oil or water to dribble out onto the pavement. If an amount of approximately 1 pint or more is collected in the wet tank, this is an indication of poor maintenance and defective equipment.

While inspecting the safety equipment of a truck, the driver should be asked to show his emergency reflectors. These are portable reflectors that may be set out on the highway to warn approaching traffic when the truck has a breakdown.

One final item that is a routine part of the inspection process is to examine the driver's license to determine if the driver is properly licensed to operate this particular combination of vehicles. Occasionally, a driver will operate a truck or truck and trailer combination while not adequately licensed to do so.

It is important to restate that inspecting equipment on a truck or truck and trailer combination is not to be done casually. It is important that the officer receive some training. It is not expected that these guidelines will equip the officer who is a novice to adequately conduct brake inspection on trucks. However, the information is offered in order to instruct in a procedure which can be learned with practice and experience. By requesting training from the department or by observing experienced officers conduct these tests, officers can develop the skill. Truck drivers themselves can also provide valuable information on the inspection of trucks.

Other safety equipment checks on a truck include fifth wheel connection and possible defects such as push rod travel on brake chambers, cracks in frame rails, etc. These items require more knowledge and training than are offered in this text. They are mentioned for the purpose of pointing out some of the obvious items that may be inspected at the roadside by an officer who has adequate knowledge and experience.

While on routine patrol, it is possible for an officer to spot vehicle equipment defects in automobiles and trucks that are being operated in traffic. The visual inspection can include the obvious such as brake lights, in the daytime as well as the night, and of course the condition of lights during darkness. When a turn signal is not activated prior to a turn, it may mean a careless driver or defective equipment. When a vehicle with streaks across the windshield is observed, defective wiper blades are usually indicated. This observation provides the officer with probable cause to believe that a vehicle defect exists, and he may stop the vehicle for further inspection.

Another "flag" that may indicate a problem is the flashing of brake lights when a vehicle is coming to a stop at a red signal or stop sign. The flashing of brake lights may indicate that the driver is pumping the brake pedal in order to build up sufficient hydraulic pressure to stop the vehicle. The vehicle could have defective brakes or a short circuit in the brake lights; either one is sufficient reason for further inspection.

The officer should develop the ability to visually inspect the obvious equipment on a vehicle in traffic by watching for proper function of lights, brakes, etc. Also, he should develop the habit of looking at tire surfaces on vehicles stopped in traffic. While waiting behind a car at a traffic signal, he may observe bald tires on the rear. This is more difficult to observe on a vehicle that is moving, but the officer should notice that rotating tires that are bald will show a different appearance than rotating tires with adequate tread. The ability to recognize this difference comes with experience.

Quite a few traffic accidents are caused by defective safety equipment on vehicles. Additionally, some traffic accidents that are caused by driver error may be magnified by equipment failure when attempting to stop or maneuver the vehicle. It is very important to protect the other motorists from the careless driver, and quite often his carelessness will be indicated through the lack of maintenance of his vehicle. It will be fairly easy to observe the signs of obvious neglect on an automobile, and when these signs are observed, immediate action should be taken to prevent the vehicle from becoming the cause or contributor in a traffic accident.

CHAPTER EIGHT

APPREHENDING SPEED VIOLATORS

THE MATERIAL in this chapter is intended to provide the reader with the necessary information to accomplish the following:
* Recognize speed violations when observing traffic
* Develop the ability to visually estimate the speed of suspected violators
* Develop the ability to accurately pace a speeding vehicle in traffic using the patrol car speedometer
* Develop the ability to accurately pace a speeding vehicle on the open highway from as far back as half a mile, using both the speedometer and the odometer

One of the most common traffic violations committed by motorists is that of violating the speed laws. The characteristics of speed violations vary, depending on the regulations of individual states. The prima facie limit, the maximum speed limit, and the basic speed law are examples of speed regulations.

The prima facie speed limit refers to the sign posted along the highway which sets the speed limit in a given area. This is one of the most common speed violations that the traffic officer will encounter. Traffic usually moves at approximately the speed limit, depending on the location, and sometimes slightly faster. An individual speed violator will be recognizable by the distance between his vehicle and other traffic as well as by the widening of the gap as he pulls away.

The maximum speed limit is set by the state legislature and

says that no vehicle shall go any faster than a given speed anywhere in the state. In recent years the 55 MPH speed limit has become a nationwide standard. Previously, individual states had varied on their maximum speed limits.

The basic speed law refers to a general section stating that anyone who drives at a speed greater than that which is reasonable or prudent, having due regard for weather, visibility, traffic on the surface, and the width of the highway, or greater than is safe for persons or property, is in violation. The basic speed law would then take effect under any conditions that were hazardous and would reduce the posted speed limit accordingly. An example is a stretch of highway, posted speed limit 45 MPH, that is covered by fog in the early morning hours. Visibility has been reduced to approximately 100 feet. It would not be safe or prudent to drive at 45 MPH under these conditions; therefore, the speed must be reduced until the driver is no longer overdriving his visibility. The same would be true if the roadway were icy or if there was a heavy rainfall, etc.

When observing traffic, an officer needs to develop the ability to recognize speed violations when he sees them. Sometimes a speeder is not exceeding the limit radically enough to stand out from the crowd. However, if the officer will study the movement of traffic, he will note that some vehicles are moving away from others almost imperceptively. Continued over a long distance, they will widen the gap and pull away from the pack. The variance between the vehicles may be 5 miles per hour or so. At other times the officer will note subtle speed violations by looking in the rearview mirror when driving in traffic. If the officer monitors his mirror, he will eventually notice a vehicle gaining on him from the rear until the driver identifies the patrol car; then the officer will see a reduction in speed. This observation in the mirror may not be sufficient to issue a traffic citation, but it would be a valid reason for stopping the vehicle to warn the driver.

One skill which is necessary for a successful traffic officer to function is the ability to visually estimate the speed of moving vehicles. One of the best ways to develop this skill is to practice observing vehicles that are moving at known speeds so that when that known movement is seen at a later time, it will be recognized as the given speed previously observed.

The speed of vehicles may be converted from miles per hour to feet per second (FPS) by multiplying 1.467 × miles per hour (MPH). Table I is a chart of speeds varying from 25 to 70 MPH and their attendant speed in feet per second (FPS). Using this as a guide, the traffic officer, equipped with a stopwatch, can set up an observation post on various highways that are posted at different speeds. Using his stopwatch to measure the time it takes for a vehicle to go between two points of known distance, he can determine the speed of the vehicle, thereby developing the ability to predict speed. This technique is not intended as an enforcement procedure, but purely for educational purposes. Whether or not it is used as an enforcement procedure will depend on the policy of the department which employs the officer or the law in the state in which he works. Even if it is illegal to use a stopwatch to measure speed for enforcement purposes, it would still be appropriate to pursue a vehicle that was determined to be speeding by this method. Once the stopwatch is put away, the officer then may use his vehicle's speedometer to pace the speeder and determine his speed in the traditional method. Having done this, he may then issue a citation based on the speedometer pace.

TABLE I

MILES PER HOUR(MPH) CONVERTED TO FEET PER SECOND (FPS)

MPH × 1.467 = FPS
25 MPH = 37 FPS
30 MPH = 44 FPS
35 MPH = 51 FPS
40 MPH = 59 FPS
45 MPH = 66 FPS
50 MPH = 73 FPS
55 MPH = 81 FPS
60 MPH = 88 FPS
65 MPH = 95 FPS
70 MPH = 103 FPS

This chapter does not devote any instruction to the use of radar or electronic timing devices for measuring speed. The technical instructions required to properly use those devices are given as part of the training when a department uses devices as part of its equipment. The manufacturer will usually provide training for departments purchasing its radar. Instead, this chapter is devoted to using more conventional methods for speed determination. Electronic devices are very beneficial in cutting down the effort and hazard in speed determination. However, it is the author's opinion that a traffic officer needs to learn more basic ways of determining speed of vehicles. This will give him a more sensitive awareness of his work and of what is happening around him on the highway.

Using the speedometer of the patrol car is one of the more basic methods of determining speed for purposes of enforcement. It is not as easy as it sounds. Officers who have not been properly instructed in pacing speed with a speedometer will quite often misread the distance, believing that they are following a vehicle at a holding pace. Depth perception is very important in pacing speed; any gain or loss of distance will affect the accuracy of the pace. I have ridden with an officer who was pacing a vehicle with his speedometer and had determined in his own mind that the vehicle was speeding. What the officer did not realize was that he was gaining on the vehicle perceptibly, and this had a contaminating effect on the pace.

It is difficult to decide when a speedometer pace is precisely on the mark. The best way I can think of is to say that when the officer is precisely pacing a vehicle at the exact speed it is traveling, he will have a subtle feeling of holding or hanging in space. He is not gaining or losing, but precisely traveling with the vehicle. If there is any creeping effect, however slight, he is gaining and, therefore, not accurately pacing. It is better to reduce speed slowly until the other vehicle is obviously pulling away. When this occurs, the officer may then increase speed by increments of 5 miles per hour until he is holding perfectly with the pace of the other car.

The speedometer on a police car used for traffic enforcement must be accurate. It is important that the speedometer be electronically calibrated no less than every ninety days. If there is an error in the speedometer, it would be reflected on a calibration chart that is posted on the dashboard within the driver's view. A speedometer which reads 60 MPH, but is actually measuring 58 MPH, will have an effect of 2 miles an hour on the end product. The 2 miles an hour may be reflected consistently across the dial or may vary. Therefore, all speeds from 25 to 60 (MPH) should be listed with the error indicated for the officer's computation.

An electric fifth wheel is the device used by some departments to calibrate the vehicles in their automotive fleet. Another method that is also being used is to have the patrol cars pass through the radar beam at various speeds in order to determine speedometer accuracy. Either method will suffice, but each must be documented. This information should go to court with the officer when he testifies on a speed violation. It is likely that the defense attorney or the prosecuting attorney will ask about the accuracy of a patrol vehicle's speedometer.

While pacing a suspected speeder, the officer needs to focus his attention on the vehicle itself and drive his vehicle in concert with it as much as possible. When he feels that he is holding exactly the pace of the other car, he may glance quickly down at his speedometer to determine the speed. He should look up again and make a positive verification that he is still holding with the other car and then glance quickly down once more at the speedometer. To concentrate on the speedometer itself, glancing up occasionally at the other car, is a tendency that is easy to develop. When working speed, an officer can easily become distracted by the device (speedometer) that is most involved in his measurement. However, the method of studying the vehicle rather than the instrument would be a more accurate determination.

It is possible to accurately pace a speeding vehicle on the open highway from as far back as half a mile or more using both the speedometer and odometer of the vehicle. The speedometer is the instrument which measures miles per hour and the odom-

Apprehending Speed Violators

eter is the counter that logs miles traveled. The odometer also has a tenth of a mile digit which would be useful in this method. If the officer observes a vehicle ahead in traffic that appears to be speeding, he should make an initial visual estimate of the vehicle's speed. Then he should accelerate to that approximate speed and concentrate on holding that speed without variation. When the suspected violator is observed passing a distinctive landmark on the highway, such as a bridge overpass, a light standard, etc., the officer should note on his pad the last 2 mile digits on the odometer and the tenth of a mile reading. For example, if the patrol vehicle odometer reads 28600.5, the officer would note 00.5 on his pad. Continuing to hold the estimated speed of the violator (in this case 70 MPH will be used), the officer waits until he passes the same landmark. At exactly that point he writes down the patrol vehicle odometer reading again. In this example the odometer reads 28600.9. Subtracting .5 from .9 leaves a distance of .4 of a mile. This means that when the officer observed the suspected violator's vehicle pass the landmark, the distance between the two cars was at least .4 of a mile. The officer continues to follow the suspected vehicle at the estimated speed and when another landmark is passed, he documents his odometer reading again. In this example, the odometer on the second landmark check reads 28601.6. When the officer reaches that landmark point, his odometer reads 28602.1. The distance between the two cars is .5 of a mile. This means that the violator is gaining or pulling away from the officer. He has gained .1 of a mile in the last mile traveled. The speed of 70 MPH, which is used in this example, would then be clearly a minimum speed for the violator. Since he is gaining or pulling away from the patrol car, we know that he is exceeding the 70 MPH figure. The officer may continue this check as many times as he feels necessary in order to verify the violator's speed. The distances indicated here are .4 of a mile and .5 of a mile between the patrol car and the violator. This method can be successful from as far back as the officer can see the vehicle. When the officer is quite a ways back from the violator's vehicle, it is probable that he will not understand how the officer was able to pace him without being closer, especially since the officer is not using radar. A quick explanation of the odometer method will make it easy for most people to understand how this is done. It is necessary for the officer to be prepared to explain the method in court, with a diagram on the blackboard if necessary, to help the judge and jury to understand the method.

The method of pacing speed with the speedometer and odometer is specifically a measurement of time and distance. The only difference between this and using a stopwatch is that a speedometer is acceptable in all locations as a device for measuring speed and a stopwatch is not. The odometer is measuring the distance over which the pace for speed takes place, and the speedometer measures the speed with which the pace takes place.

Using the odometer to pace speed is more effective on an open highway than on city streets because of the freedom of time in recording landmark checks. It would be possible over a series of city blocks to use this method in city traffic, but the officer's attention would be distracted from his driving to the point of being hazardous. Therefore, it is not recommended under these circumstances.

CHAPTER NINE

EMERGENCY VEHICLE OPERATION

THE MATERIAL in this chapter is intended to provide the reader with the necessary information to accomplish the following:
- Recognize the effect of the patrol car as a power symbol
- Recognize the extreme hazards involved in driving a patrol car during the high speed pursuit of a violator
- Recognize the extreme hazards involved in responding to an emergency call with lights and siren
- Understand and control siren hypnosis

The presence of a marked police vehicle has a noticeable effect on motorists in traffic. It has sometimes been referred to as "halo effect." People are on their best behavior when they are faced with the presence of authority. The officer operating a police vehicle in traffic will see evidence of deference to his position by the way people drive. If he is waiting to turn left at an intersection, usually a driver coming from the opposite direction, who has the right of way, will stop and wave the officer on. If he is waiting to come out of a driveway, someone will usually provide a break in traffic to allow him to do so. Let him try the same maneuvers in his own personal vehicle, and he will find that very few people will respond in the same manner.

When a marked police car enters a freeway or turnpike from an entrance ramp, a distinct change in the driving habits of other motorists will be seen. It is like the reaction of a school of fish when they observe the presence of a shark; they proceed very carefully and spend a lot of their time watching him. If an officer finds himself behind another vehicle for a long period of time, he may be paying little or no attention to that particular car. However, if the driver of the other vehicle were to be interviewed, he would swear that the officer was "following him," looking for an opportunity to pull him over for a traffic infraction.

It is this paranoia among motorists that makes the marked police vehicle highly visible and a definite symbol of power during its normal driving operations. Unfortunately, the effect of a patrol car does not extend far enough ahead when involved in a high speed pursuit or in response to an emergency call. It is during high speed driving that the officer wants his presence to be known and wants to have the special right-of-way as far ahead as possible. It seems as though the operation of the vehicle during normal patrol causes a great deal of effect on other traffic, yet when the vehicle is driven rapidly with lights flashing and siren in operation, people almost resist yielding the right-of-way or do not notice the vehicle until the last minute. This phenomenon makes high speed operation of an emergency vehicle very hazardous.

When a police officer attempts to stop the vehicle for a violation and is faced with a high speed pursuit, he is immediately exposed to a number of hazards inherent in this operation. The first is his tendency to focus his attention specifically on the other vehicle being pursued. The narrowing of vision that occurs often blocks out the things he needs to see on the periphery of his vision such as cross traffic, pedestrians, and so forth. It is only with a great deal of experience and training that an officer develops the ability to widen his vision and to become aware of many other things besides his quarry.

While seated inside of a police car that is in pursuit of a violator, the officer is intensely aware of the sound of his siren and of his lights in operation. It seems as though the sound of the siren fills the interior of the patrol car and creates the illusion to the officer that it can be heard everywhere. However, the siren has definite limits in reaching the ears of motorists driving inside of closed vehicles. If a motorist is proceeding down the highway with his windows closed and his radio playing, it is unlikely that he will hear a siren until the emergency vehicle is almost on his bumper. Usually, people become aware of the emergency vehicle by glimpsing the flashing lights in their rearview mirrors or by noticing the behavior of their fellow motorists who are pulling to the side of the road. Human behavior is quite interesting in the way that different people react to an approaching emergency vehicle, especially one that is approaching from the rear. If the vehicle is clearly identified as a police car, the motorist usually first thinks of himself as being the target of the officer's lights and siren. This will sometimes cause a preoccupation with such thoughts as, "I wonder what I did," and slow the reaction time for yielding to the emergency vehicle.

People who observe the approach of a high speed emergency vehicle pursuing another car will usually gladly yield the right-of-way and become excited with the spirit of the chase. When the pursued vehicle is driving at a high rate of speed and passes unsafely through traffic, they are quick to cheer the officer and give him the road. By facing the direction from which he is coming, they have a better viewpoint and can more easily evaluate the situation in order to yield in time.

Numerous tests have been conducted under controlled conditions to determine the effect of the siren on persons driving in normal traffic, and it was determined, using all types of sirens, that most of them were ineffective in being heard by motorists inside of closed vehicles. While approaching a closed vehicle from the rear during a controlled test, the driver of the front vehicle was to signal with his headlights when he first perceived the sound of the siren. In most cases the headlights were turned on when the approaching emergency vehicle was within no more than two car lengths to the rear; so much for the effectiveness of a siren.

When a high speed pursuit takes place in a downtown area, with medium traffic, the officer has a tremendous responsibility in protecting other motorists from the results of the pursuit. His siren is a continuous order for the fleeing driver to yield, but it is also a warning to those ahead that an extreme hazard is coming at high speed. Too often the chase takes both the fleeing driver and the officer onto the wrong side of the road and around corners where they cannot see what is in the roadway until they are upon it. It is an unresolved question whether the officer should continue his pursuit "no matter what" and dog the individual who is fleeing until he either submits by pulling over or loses control of his vehicle or, on the other hand, make a conscious decision to break off the chase because of the extreme hazard to innocent bystanders. Some police departments have policies which dictate the officer's conduct during a pursuit, and some of those policies direct the officer to break off the chase if he finds himself approaching traffic that may be affected by the high speed pursuit. Other jurisdictions believe that any resulting traffic accidents involving innocent parties are the direct responsibility of the fleeing motorist and will charge him with additional violations.

The "spirit of the chase" is one of the exciting aspects of police work. It is truly difficult for a young officer, who enjoys the excitement of his work, to resist the lure of joining in a pursuit that comes by his location. The difficulty with having every available officer become a part of a high speed pursuit is mainly with the incredible traffic problem that it creates. By considering one fleeing vehicle being pursued by up to fifteen or twenty police cars, one can imagine the problems that may result.

In one situation that I can recall, the local police department was in pursuit of a suspected burglary suspect. While sitting at an intersection and listening to the approaching sirens, it soon became apparent to me that the suspect was winning the race. Since I was driving a high powered pursuit vehicle, it seemed to be my duty to join in and capture the culprit. As soon as the suspect's vehicle roared through the intersection where I was stopped, against the red light, I waited my turn to enter the chase. It seemed as if I were waiting for a train to pass a crossing, because I counted 22 police cars which went by me before I had an opportunity to join in the line. Due to the superior design of the vehicle I was driving, I ultimately reached the head of the line and closed the distance on the vehicle which was pursued.

Despite my presence, he continued to flee, and I was unable to convince him to stop by staying to the rear. I pulled alongside, but this movement also had no effect. Finally, feeling very frustrated, I pulled around the vehicle and in front of it, blocking its path. Eventually, the driver slowed down because he was unable to pass me and was forced to stop. Looking back on the incident with many more years of experience, I shudder to think of the incredible hazard which I created for myself and my partner. We exited our patrol car with weapons drawn, and the suspect driver engaged his vehicle again and went around us, leaving us standing in the roadway. The delay was just enough for the other vehicles in the pursuit to catch up, and the chase continued. Shortly thereafter, I heard the sound of one gunshot, and within a very short time the chase was terminated. The next day the police chief of the department who initiated the pursuit did an investigation. He found that a total of thirty police vehicles from various departments were involved in the chase of one suspect. Two of the police vehicles were involved in traffic accidents as they roared through intersections attempting to close on the quarry. One of the officers who was involved in a traffic accident did not stop at the scene and continued, technically becoming a suspect himself of hit and run. The gunshot which I described earlier had been fired by one of the pursuing officers in an effort to disable the fleeing suspect. It took some time to locate where the bullet had gone because it did not strike the suspect's vehicle. It was later found in the engine block of one of the pursuing police cars.

Public reaction to this parade of emergency vehicles was not good. The local newspaper printed a lengthy editorial in which the police were chastised for being so zealous in their efforts to apprehend one individual that they caused hazard, minor injury, and property damage to many other people.

The California Highway Patrol (CHP) has a policy on pursuits. First, if the pursuit is initiated by another police agency, the CHP has instructed their officers not to become involved in the chase unless specifically requested to do so by the initiating agency. Second, when a pursuit results from the actions of a

CHP officer, the number of CHP vehicles permitted to take part in the chase is limited to two patrol units and a supervisor. This eliminates the possibility of such a circus and comedy of errors as I have just described. The supervisor who joins the chase has the control and can deploy other units, if necessary, by radio.

When the incredible demands on a police officer who is driving his vehicle in a high speed pursuit are considered, it is amazing that more serious accidents do not occur. He has a large dose of adrenaline pumping through his system, based on the excitement of the event. This puts a strain on his heart and on his whole system. He must call upon his very best skills in operating a 4,000 pound guided missile that is hurtling down the highway at speeds quite often in excess of 100 miles per hour. He must also operate his radio in order to notify his dispatcher and other units of his location, and he must look ahead of the violator's vehicle searching for cross traffic and other hazards that must be avoided. If the violator's vehicle becomes involved in a traffic accident or suddenly pulls over, he must now respond, stopping his vehicle short of colliding with the wreckage or overshooting the stopped vehicle. When the chase does terminate and he exits from his patrol car, usually his hands are shaking and his mental and physical condition is extremely agitated, based on the tremendous pressure of the chase. Sometimes it is necessary for a second officer to restrain him from striking the person who has just led him through such an experience.

Based on what I have just described, I would like to offer a warning to novice officers when they find themselves involved in their first vehicle pursuits. Having read this chapter, you have information that will prepare you for what is to come. Take your time, even if it means losing one or two. The experience you will gain will eventually make you a winner. Talk to veteran officers who have been involved in numerous pursuits during their career, and ask them to tell you about some of the bizarre events that have occurred as a result of the chase. It will help you to develop some very important data for your mental computer and perhaps to avoid unnecessary injury or even death.

When operating an emergency vehicle in response to an emergency call, the tendency is to drive too fast. The officer is aware of the power symbol of his patrol car with its bright emergency lights and what seems to be a very loud siren, and he is stimulated by the excitement of the pending emergency. It is difficult not to become enraptured by the power of the situation and subconsciously consider oneself to be invincible. Observing the results of the involvement of emergency vehicles in traffic accidents will probably be necessary before the message is absorbed.

When responding to an emergency call, the officer needs to remember that his services are desperately needed by someone in trouble. If he becomes involved in a traffic accident en route to provide that important service, he will not be able to help the people who have called for him. Additionally, he will have created a monetary and possibly a tragic problem for those with whom he has collided. When a police car is involved in a traffic accident, many people will pass judgement against the officer when they drive by. It is expected by the general public that police personnel will use superior ability, training, and experience in driving their emergency vehicles under emergency conditions. They are quick to criticize when a police officer exhibits human tendencies, like their own, and makes a mistake.

It is possible for the officer to respond to an emergency and to arrive safely and quickly if he will concentrate most of his faculties on the trip rather than on the arrival. It will be necessary for him to do some preplanning in his mind about how he will handle the emergency that will be waiting for him, and not to do so would be a mistake. However, this is an area in which training prevails. If the officer has been taught to deal with traffic accidents or other emergencies upon arrival, he will need less time to concentrate on his plan. Any tendency to drive fast should be reduced. Movement may seem agonizingly slow, but a safe arrival will be more likely.

Some police departments in larger locations, which have experienced many accidents while responding to emergency calls, have placed limits on the speed that their officers travel. It is unfortunate that such limits must be placed when the officers possess the capability of exercising good judgement.

A phenomenon which occurs when operating an emergency vehicle with red lights and siren is called "siren hypnosis." Since the siren noise level is its highest inside the vehicle, the officer will tend to become fascinated with the siren, and as it climbs to its peak he will tend to press down on the accelerator. It is difficult to recognize siren hypnosis in oneself unless one preprograms one's thinking to look for it. The exhilarating experience of rocketing through traffic and having all heads turn in the officer's direction, coupled with the excitement of the event which awaits his arrival, makes siren hypnosis a very likely occurrence.

Conscious thought, preplanning, awareness of what is happening around him, concern for his fellow man, and experience will all contribute to the officer's ability in operating an emergency vehicle during trying conditions.

CHAPTER TEN

RECOGNIZING COMMON DRIVING VIOLATIONS OBSERVED DURING PATROL

THE MATERIAL in this chapter is intended to provide the reader with the necessary information to accomplish the following:
- Develop the hunter instinct
- Develop a personal driving pattern while on patrol
- Identify the elements of the most common rules-of-the-road violations
- Develop observation techniques which will alert the officer when a driving violation is committed in his presence
- Monitor personal driving habits while on patrol

Part of the police officer's job is to detect misconduct and take action to correct it — the act of "enforcing" the law. Some consider it a negative aspect of police work to spend one's time catching people committing traffic infractions. There is some resentment toward this part of the police traffic control function. Perhaps it is because anyone could be a recipient of a traffic citation. Therefore, there is a sense of fear behind the question, "Why aren't you out catching real criminals?" In fact, more lives are lost as a result of careless driving than any other "crime." The officer who is aggressive in his efforts to apprehend drivers for violating traffic regulations is likely to have a definite effect on the number of lives lost from traffic accidents. Since the term *accident* refers to an action that is the result of no intentional wrongdoing, the traffic officer is seeking out subjects who are merely careless.

In order for a traffic officer to be successful in observing traffic violations within his presence, he must actively look for them. He is a hunter and his quarry is the traffic violator. The officer must develop a hunter's instinct in seeking this quarry. He may feel a sense of satisfaction that is justified when he takes enforcement action against a traffic violator who has committed a hazardous driving act. The contents of this chapter are designed to provide the basic elements and some guidelines in recognizing a traffic violation that has occurred in the officer's presence.

The traffic officer's personal driving pattern during patrol duty will be responsible for his successful observation of violators. If he is operating his patrol vehicle in traffic and becomes part of that traffic by the way he drives, it will be easy to think of other things. If, instead, he varies his driving so that it is different from the pace of routine traffic, he is more likely to be aware of the driving pattern of others. This can be accomplished in different ways. The officer is engaged in an activity known as traffic supervision, which means that he is observing the driving of others for the purpose of obtaining compliance with the law. The observation of traffic can be conducted both while becoming part of the traffic flow and also while standing still at the roadside.

When patrolling a through highway upon which traffic flows for long distances at a sustained speed, the officer may vary his speed so that at times he is being passed by traffic and at times he is moving slightly faster than the flow. When driving slower than the pack of vehicles, it is best to do so in the right-hand lane so that traffic can pass safely to the left. The effect of the presence of the patrol car will be mainly to slow the flow of traffic. Some people will drive even less than the speed limit in order to avoid receiving a speeding ticket. Most of the officer's observation under these circumstances will be in the rearview mirror observing the conduct of motorists who have not yet detected his presence. He will see people approaching rapidly from the rear until they notice the presence of the patrol car, at which time they will usually slow down along with everyone else. The fact that he has observed that vehicle proceeding faster than the flow of traffic for a short distance may be sufficient cause to stop the vehicle and have a conversation with the driver. Also observed in the rearview mirror will be lane changes that may take place without signals or sufficient clearance.

When stationary observation is being conducted, the location of the patrol car may or may not be in plain view. This will be governed by the policy of the police agency that employs the officer. It has been said in earlier chapters that lying in wait out of sight has been the cause of considerable resentment on the part of some citizens. However, it is a very effective method for seeing people at their worst. If they are not aware that a police officer is observing their driving action, they may very well commit a driving violation. If the officer is in plain view, the motorists will probably be on their best behavior, but it is likely that the good behavior will last only as long as they think they are being observed. When members of the California Highway Patrol were involved in the practice of parking on entrance ramps to California freeways, out of view of the passing traffic, they were very successful in detecting and arresting speed violators. That practice was changed by a new policy of highly visible, in-view patrol. The philosophy behind the new policy was to deter violations in advance rather than take enforcement action after they occur. The policy was lauded by many members of the press and the general public as being a positive act, rather than a negative one. The results were a drop in citations and a feeling of resentment on the part of the traffic officers.

When a sampling of motorists was questioned as to the effect (positive or negative) of a highway patrol car sitting on entrance ramps, the results were interesting. The majority of people admitted that the possibility of that patrol car being at the next exit ramp kept them from exceeding the speed limit on many occasions. It was the unseen hazard of a traffic officer and a citation book that kept these motorists in line. Others said that it created a very negative feeling in them when they observed the police hiding, "just waiting for a chance to get me." The issue is one for debate and again must be resolved by the policy of the department with which the officer is employed.

The most common rules-of-the-road violations will be discussed herein with some comments on how to recognize them and some of the basic elements required. Previous reference has been made to automotive equipment violations, and quite often they will be discovered when making a stop for another driving act.

Signs, Signals, and Markings

The tricolored traffic signal is a common device encountered in most communities. The colors are universal, in that green means go, amber or yellow means caution, and red requires a stop. In some jurisdictions the green light not only permits traffic to proceed, but *requires* traffic to proceed on the green. In those areas it is not the option for the driver to remain stopped through a green light. He must proceed, and his failure to do so will impede other traffic. The red light violation is one which is commonly the cause of traffic accidents. Determining that a red light violation has occurred in the officer's presence requires several things. First, the officer must be in a position to see the color of the light that is seen by the motorist who is the suspected violator. Sitting at a broadside angle to the intersection and observing a green light does not suffice in many courts to convict a person who crosses through that intersection. The officer is acting upon an assumption that the violator is observing a red signal because the signal in the officer's direction was green. If a vehicle is observed proceeding through an intersection across the officer's path and he has a green light, it would be useful to immediately look at the color of the light faced by the driver in question.

Another point when dealing with red signal violations is whether the vehicle was behind the crosswalk or the limit line after the light changed. This is the point of argument that arises in most cases involving a red light. Some locations permit a vehicle to proceed through the intersection if it entered on the amber light even though the light changed to red prior to completing the traverse of the intersection. Different drivers possess different timing and awareness and will quite often think that they have the yellow light when in fact it is red. The officer needs to be able to see the position of the vehicle behind the limit line or crosswalk when the light changed in order to determine a violation.

Stop signs are in a similar category. People perceive the term *stop* to mean different things. Some believe that if they have slowed their vehicle down to 5 or 10 miles an hour it is sufficient to comply as a stop. This is not the case according to the law. The vehicle must cease all forward motion and do so behind the limit line or prior to entering the intersection in order to comply with the stop sign. It will be the case at some time in the traffic officer's career to notice a vehicle proceeding across an intersection at such a speed as to convince the officer that it could not have possibly stopped at the crosswalk or limit line. For the vehicle to have achieved such speed after making a stop would have required incredible acceleration. The officer may stop the vehicle and proceed to warn the driver based on what he believes has occurred, but it would not be legal or correct to issue a citation without having fully observed the violation itself.

Some jurisdictions have pedestrian signals that consist of signs that flash the words *Walk, Wait,* or *Don't Walk.* These operate independently of the tricolor signal. Usually, they are installed in locations where traffic volume is high enough to require the clearing of pedestrians from the intersection before the green light in order not to impede vehicular traffic. Pedestrians will usually respond to these signals based on two things: first, their own need for law-abiding conduct, and second, the fear of receiving a traffic citation. Some jurisdictions make no effort to control pedestrians; consequently, a lot of pedestrians will be seen crossing against pedestrian signals as well as tricolor signals. The result is usually a higher frequency of auto versus pedestrian accidents in that jurisdiction. If the officer is unable to get through traffic to make an enforcement contact with a pedestrian, he should remember that use of the public address system on the patrol car may be just as effective.

Right-of-Way

There are a number of variations of the requirement to yield right-of-way to others. The variations occur depending on the jurisdiction and local laws. One of the most common points of contention is the uncontrolled intersection. The common rule for two vehicles approaching at right angles to an uncontrolled intersection is that the right-of-way belongs to the vehicle which arrived first; thus, the controversy. If both vehicles arrive simultaneously, the right-of-way goes to the vehicle on the right. This means that if the reader is one of the simultaneous vehicles and the other vehicle is to his left, he (the reader) has the right of way. If the other vehicle is to his right, he must yield. Determining the right-of-way requires the officer to be in a position to observe the approach of both vehicles. Usually this will occur while stationary.

Another commonly occurring area of right-of-way violation (and the cause of many accidents) is the left-turning vehicle at an intersection. The right-of-way normally belongs to through traffic, and when a vehicle is attempting to turn left, against that flow of traffic, the driver must remain stopped until there is adequate clearance to safely make his left turn. Occasionally, drivers who are proceeding straight ahead will slow down and wave the turning driver to proceed, thereby giving up their right-of-way. Unfortunately, when there is more than one lane of traffic, the driver who waves the turning vehicle on can give up his own right-of-way but has no control over the next lane, and the result can be a traffic accident. One commonly employed tactic is that of the left-turning driver who watches for the change of signal and then accelerates rapidly in order to make his turn through the intersection before through traffic can start. This quite often causes rapid braking and sometimes a traffic accident. Such a movement would be subject to enforcement action.

Some intersections are controlled by "yield" signs, which means that when approaching the intersection and observing the sign, the right-of-way must be yielded to cross traffic. This is not the same as a stop sign, but does require a considerable reduction in speed. Some locations have even legislated a maximum speed of 15 miles per hour through the intersection when faced with a yield sign. Therefore, the officer may observe a vehicle proceeding through and, although no cars are approaching, the speed of the vehicle will constitute a violation.

It is sometimes difficult to determine when a vehicle stopped at a stop sign may proceed. If there is a continuous flow of traffic on a cross street, the law usually states that the driver may proceed only when it is safe to do so after having made the stop. This is a judgement factor which the officer must make when he sees a driver proceed from a stop sign into the path of oncoming traffic. The driver may have been sitting at the intersection for a long period of time and is motivated by frustration. The officer's observation must determine if a right-of-way violation has occurred.

Another right-of-way situation which is of special interest to the officer involves traffic which must yield to emergency vehicles. If the fire department is responding to a fire and is having difficulty getting through traffic, the officer should consider taking enforcement action against any vehicles observed failing to yield a right-of-way by pulling to the right and stopping. The same is true of an ambulance or other authorized emergency vehicle. By taking enforcement action against these drivers, the officer is setting the example for others who observe the stop by letting them know this violation is serious. It also reemphasizes the need to yield the right-of-way to emergency vehicles so that when he is responding to an emergency call more people will be likely to yield to him.

Turning and Signaling

Turning movements are identifiable as violations when the vehicle is in an improper position for the turn. For the most part, right turns must be made as close as practicable to the right-hand edge of a curb and left turns as close as practicable to the left-hand side of the roadway or the center line. Many locations have designated turn lanes for right and left turns which must be used by turning vehicles. Any turning movement, including lane changes, requires a signal. Quite often drivers will omit the signal because of their haste, and this is an area ripe for enforcement.

As with right or left turning movements, u-turns may be controlled by posted signs either permitting or prohibiting them. The officer needs to become familiar with his beat so that he knows where such turns are permitted or prohibited in order to recognize a violation when it occurs. Any turning movement can be unsafe if the position of the vehicle causes a hazard to other traffic.

Driving, Overtaking, and Passing

In America, it is required in all states that vehicles drive on the right half of the roadway. In some countries in Europe the opposite is true and the left-hand side of the roadway is used. It is usually apparent when someone is failing to drive on the proper side of the road, especially when he meets another driver coming on the driver's own side. Occasionally, people who live in an area with many one-way streets will develop the habit of driving to the left, and when they are on a two-way street they may lapse into this habit, creating quite a hazard.

Some highways are divided either by barriers, curbs, or markings so that traffic in opposite directions is separated. Since paint is cheaper than concrete, quite often the center divider will consist of painted markings which constitute, from the legal standpoint, just as much of a barrier as a concrete curb. However, it is easier to drive over paint than concrete, so there is the temptation for motorists to turn across the divider when it suits their convenience. The officer needs to be aware of the markings on the road surface in order to recognize this violation when it occurs.

Slow vehicles, that is vehicles being operated more slowly than the speed limits, will sometimes be a source of frustration for other drivers who will pass when it is not safe to do so. When this occurs, the officer needs to look at both the slow-moving vehicles and the passing vehicles to determine if he may have two violations instead of one. Some states have laws which prohibit slow-moving vehicles from impeding the traffic.

Driving within the designated traffic lane is a common requirement. When a vehicle straddles the line between its lane and the next, the driver is failing to drive within his lane and in many jurisdictions is committing a traffic violation. Such driving conduct may also be an indication of an intoxicated driver or of other problems which need to be considered when stopping this driver.

In various jurisdictions, passing to the right is permitted under certain conditions. If there is an unoccupied lane to the right of the vehicle which the driver wishes to pass, he may legally use that lane in passing. Other jurisdictions do not permit passing on the right under any circumstances.

In those areas where passing on the right is permitted, there is usually a prohibition against using the right-hand shoulder or driving off the main, traveled portion of the roadway. This violation will frequently occur when heavy commuter traffic is moving slowly and a frustrated driver sees an opportunity to gain time by traveling down the right-hand shoulder and reaching the next intersection ahead of everyone else. This may be a difficult violation to enforce, depending upon whether the officer's location in traffic allows him to apprehend the driver.

When working in an area where there is a prevalent act, such as during a heavy commute period, the officer may position himself off to the right-hand shoulder so that the act of passing in that area is not possible due to the location of the patrol vehicle.

On the California freeway system, in the Los Angeles area, the morning commute traffic is extremely heavy. The temptation to drive down the paved shoulder to reach an exit ramp rather than sitting in stop-and-go traffic for several more minutes is fairly common among some motorists. Members of the California Highway Patrol who are operating solo motorcycle units have been successful in dealing with this problem by parking their motorcycles on the shoulder in direct line with a highway lamp post. They are in clear view of passing traffic and complying with the department's high visibility patrol policy, but by lining the motorcycle up with the post, are not readily visible to the vehicle that is coming from the rear down the shoulder.

When the officer sees in his rearview mirror the approach of one or more vehicles passing on the right shoulder, he can step off his motorcycle and hold up his hand, stopping those vehicles for enforcement action. Due to the solid line of cars on the freeway they are unable to escape by getting back into traffic. Quite often three or four vehicles will be cited at once.

Following too Closely

When people "tailgate" others by riding their rear bumpers, a rear-end collision may occur. This behavior may be a sign of a harried driver who is frustrated with the traffic flow and wants to force his way through. He will intimidate the drivers ahead by applying pressure until they move aside to let him pass. Others drive this way unconsciously and are not aware of the hazard they create.

The average reaction time of most people is approximately three fourths of a second. This means that it takes approximately three fourths of a second to perceive the danger ahead and to get the body to respond by applying the brakes. During that three-fourths second, the vehicle is continuing to travel at the same speed as before while the one ahead may be decelerating rapidly or already stopped.

Table II shows what the speed in feet per second (FPS) is at various miles per hour (MPH) readings. This information may be useful in explaining the hazard of the act of following too close

TABLE II
AVERAGE REACTION TIME

MPH × 1.1 = ¾ FPS
25 MPH = 28 FPS
30 MPH = 33 FPS
35 MPH = 39 FPS
40 MPH = 44 FPS
45 MPH = 50 FPS
50 MPH = 55 FPS
55 MPH = 61 FPS
60 MPH = 66 FPS
65 MPH = 72 FPS
70 MPH = 77 FPS

to a violator or in testifying in court.

A suggested rule of thumb in gauging safe following distances in traffic is approximately one car length (17–20 ft.) for each 10 MPH of speed. Anything less is courting disaster.

Some of the guidelines noted in this chapter are very routine, but a new traffic officer will find some difficulty in actually recognizing a violation unless he tunes himself to look for the elements. The need to understand what one is seeing is very important in traffic law enforcement. The endless flow of traffic, day in and day out, does have a tendency to lull one into a sense of monotony. However, if the traffic officer tunes his senses to be aware of the subtle differences in driving behavior, he will soon detect many acts which are violations and which are potentially accident-causing movements. He should remember the hunter instinct which was discussed in the beginning of this chapter. Successful hunters in the woods are those who are able to determine the presence of game where others would swear the forests were empty. The traffic officer must have the ability to see through the "forest" of apparently normal traffic patterns and observe the "game" that is invisible to others.

The officer's driving habits while operating a marked patrol car are important. He is a member of society who is willing to "call" people on their transgressions while driving vehicles. Therefore, it is necessary for him to set a proper example in his own driving habits. Only when he is responding to an emergency or pursuing a violator should he take advantage of his position. Either case calls for the use of emergency lights and perhaps a siren. The contradiction here is that when attempting to close the gap on an observed violator who is ahead of him in traffic, the officer may have to make some rapid movements; the use of emergency lights or siren would alert the violator and allow him to succeed in eluding arrest. Deciding when to do this is again a judgement factor based on experience. Some patrol cars are equipped with emergency lights that may be illuminated in one direction only, as opposed to all directions, which means that the officer might display flashing lights to the rear. This would notify other motorists of the official nature of his driving without alerting the violator ahead. People will complain about the officer who abuses his position in order to drive fast for what, to them, may be no apparent reason. It is important for the officer to be aware of his actions at all times and to avoid becoming a violator himself.

CHAPTER ELEVEN

FELONY STOPS AND ROADBLOCKS

THE MATERIAL in this chapter is intended to provide the reader with the necessary information to accomplish the following:
- Execute a safe felony stop
- Recognize the need for felony stop tactics versus routine procedure
- Define the elements of an effective roadblock in terms of manpower and equipment
- Deploy manpower and equipment in a roadblock situation at various locations, including two- and four-lane highways
- Use a countywide roadblock plan with multiple law enforcement agencies in concert.

A felony stop is a dangerous situation. It is the coming together of the police with known or suspected felons who are traveling in an automobile. While occupying the vehicle, the suspected felons have the advantage of mobility and cover. An officer who makes the stop knows in advance that he has a potentially explosive situation. It is important to develop a procedure in his own mind before making such a stop. If the department has written guidelines, then they should be followed. Contained in this chapter are some items of discussion and some ideas that may improve existing procedure. If no procedure exists at this time, these guidelines will suffice in giving basic information about dealing with a felony stop.

When stopping a vehicle that is involved in a felony crime, the officer knows that he may face resistance in making the arrest. He also should know that the probability of gunfire can be very high in felony situations; therefore, it is essential that he avoid exposing himself to fire at all times. In previous chapters the procedure for making a routine traffic stop was discussed and the officer's approach to the vehicle was outlined. In a felony stop the officer should not approach the vehicle on foot. He must remain behind the protection of his patrol car in a position that will provide him with maximum cover from gunfire, give a clear view of the suspect vehicle, and a clear field of fire for himself. The patrol vehicle provides an excellent means of cover. If the patrol vehicle is angled slightly to the left upon approaching the rear of the suspect vehicle, the body of the patrol car will give maximum protection. The officer who is driving should exit the vehicle only to a point behind his door so that he can see movement in the other car. The partner officer also will be fairly well protected if he remains behind his door, or if he wishes more substantial cover, he may hastily exit and take up a position overlooking the right rear fender. This places the body of the vehicle between him and the suspects and still allows him a clear view and field of fire. The driver officer should then give loud and clear verbal commands that will control their movements to the occupants of the felony vehicle. A public address system is the best way to do this. The human voice amplified by an electronic means will dominate psychologically.

The first command that should be given is, "All occupants of the red Ford freeze. This is the police." The next command, "All occupants of the red Ford place your hands behind your head and lace your fingers." The next command, "Driver of the red Ford, with your left hand remove the keys from the ignition and throw them out your window." The purpose of this movement is to disable the vehicle from further flight. By having the keys tossed out the window, they will probably land in the traffic lane, making them difficult to retrieve in a hurry.

The next problem is removing everyone from the vehicle safely. This should not be attempted until sufficient backup has

Felony Stops and Roadblocks

★ — police vehicle
⊗ — location of officer
✳ — lighted flare
↑ — vehicle direction

Figure 2. Felony stop position for single police unit providing maximum cover, visibility, and field of fire for the officers.

arrived. Everyone should be kept in place with their hands behind their heads so they are visible until assistance arrives. When the backup units arrive at the location, it is important that they also receive the same protection from their units. Therefore, it is not recommended that on a felony situation the backup unit park directly to the rear of the primary unit. Instead the officers should park to the side in a fan formation, even if it means blocking a traffic lane. Using the emergency lights to warn approaching traffic will be sufficient. It is better to block the traffic lane and protect approaching traffic from driving alongside of the vehicle anyway. In the event of gunfire, passing traffic would be exposed, and if this can be avoided the situation will be safer.

Once sufficient backup has arrived, the original officer in control should continue his commands as follows, "Driver, with your left hand reach outside your door and open it with the outside door handle." Second command, "Step out of the vehicle with your hands still on your head and continue facing to the front." Third command, "With your left foot, kick the door closed." The purpose of this is to make it difficult for anyone to exit the vehicle suddenly while the officer is still dealing with this one suspect. Fourth command, "Walking backwards, come to a point near the left rear fender and step to your right between the cars." The purpose here is to maneuver the subject so that he is between the patrol car and his vehicle. He should be moved all the way to the right so that he can make room for the others to join him. Once he is at the extreme right side of his vehicle's rear, the fifth command is, "Kneel down, facing the front, cross your ankles." Crossing of the ankles makes it more difficult to get up from a kneeling position.

Once the suspect is in place, he is then easily covered with weapons and can be kept in sight while the other subjects are removed. By placing him in a kneeling position, the officer is giving him some protection from gunfire that may start while he is there. It would not be appropriate to shoot him only because he is involved with the others in the vehicle, in the event that gunfire is exchanged. Therefore, by putting him in a kneel-

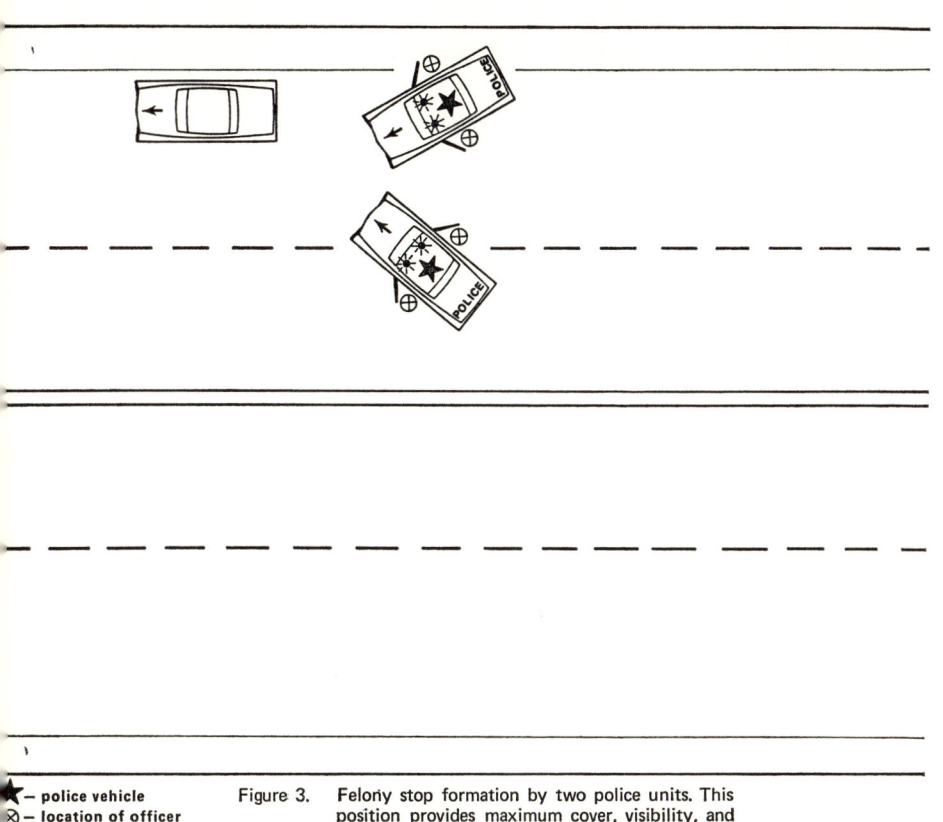

Felony Stops and Roadblocks 95

★ — police vehicle
⊗ — location of officer
⚑ — lighted flare
➤ — vehicle direction

Figure 3. Felony stop formation by two police units. This position provides maximum cover, visibility, and clear field of fire for both units.

Figure 3.

ing position, the officer is lowering the suspect's visibility and vulnerability.

The officer should continue to follow this procedure with others in the vehicle, having them exit from the left side so they may be clearly visible, not only to himself, but to the backup unit that is sitting to his left in the traffic lane. Taking the subjects one at a time allows him to maintain control of the situation and does not give them a chance to collaborate or to attack suddenly as a group. The suspects should be lined up between the cars in a kneeling position.

Once it appears that all subjects have been removed from the vehicle, the officer should remain where he is. Using the public address system again, he should give the following command, "You in the vehicle, open the door on the left side, and come out with your hands on your head." The purpose of this command is to deal with the possibility of a hidden subject who has remained in the vehicle and is waiting an opportunity to flee or open fire. By using the bluff that he knows the subject is there, the officer may cause him to surrender. If no one is there, nothing is lost by this tactic.

When no response is received from the vehicle, the officer should direct one of his associates to handle the handcuffing of the subjects on the ground. Other officers may toss him their handcuffs so there are sufficient restraint devices to control the subjects. With only one officer making the approach, the subjects are still under maximum control of the firepower from the remaining units. As he handcuffs the subjects from the rear, the approach officer should then lean them forward with their heads on the ground so they are now in a kneeling position with their weight forward on their heads. This keeps them immobile and at a low profile until ready for transport.

When he has completed the handcuffing, the advance officer should then approach the vehicle with his weapon drawn and place his hand on the rear quarter panel on the right side to feel for movement. He should then approach cautiously, looking into the rear window on the right side and then the right front window to ascertain if anyone else is in the vehicle. The possibility of a suspect hiding in the trunk should not be overlooked. This has occurred in past situations, and on at least one occasion has been fatal for a police officer who opened the trunk expecting to find contraband and instead found a suspect with a loaded shotgun.

Traffic officers are called upon to provide roadblock service when a crime has occurred and suspects are fleeing in automobiles. Knowing the territory will assist in choosing a location for a roadblock. If the agency has a preexisting plan, roadblock locations will have been chosen in advance for covering key intersections that are natural escape routes. Later in this chapter, a countywide roadblock plan will be discussed and this procedure explained. When setting up a roadblock on a two-lane highway, or at any location, it is desirable to have at least two police units at the scene. It is possible to accomplish a roadblock with less than two units, but not as effective.

The patrol vehicle should be located at a quartering angle heading in the general direction that the suspect vehicle may be traveling, turned slightly so that the broadside view of the patrol car is seen from the approach being covered. This will make it easier for identification of the police unit. The emergency lights on the patrol car should be in use at this time to further identify it and to assist in attracting the attention of approaching traffic. Traffic on the approach direction should be further warned to slow down and be prepared to stop by the use of a flare pattern. The flares should be angled away from the edge of the road leading past the front of the patrol vehicle. This will channel traffic past the front of the vehicle and allow an officer, who is out of his car and standing to the right front, to observe vehicles and occupants as they pass.

The same situation is appropriate on a four-lane road. The purpose of the flares will be to channel traffic down to one lane, which will restrict the flow and give the observing officers an opportunity to examine the identity of people in the vehicles. If the officer wishes to physically inspect identification and persons, he may wish to use flares across the traffic lane so that traffic will be required to stop and proceed one at a time.

The term *roadblock* is not entirely accurate. Correct police procedure is not to actually block the road or bar passage with a physical device. Actually, a roadblock is more of an observation post with some traffic control initiated to slow traffic. If a large truck or other obstacle were placed across the road so that a fleeing suspect had no alternative except to collide with the object, it would become a distasteful situation and involve a great deal of legal and moral repercussion. The police function can be just as effective by limiting access and passage and establishing an official presence that will probably deter further flight. If flight is not deterred, it will at least be monitored, and pursuit can take place in short order.

The second patrol unit should be parked across the street and facing in the opposite direction to the flow of traffic being monitored. The reason for this is to anticipate that a suspect vehicle approaching and observing the roadblock in place will possibly make a u-turn and go back in the direction from which he came. For the officer who is manning the primary unit to get into his car and make his way through traffic in order to pursue the suspect will take considerable time and may result in a traffic accident. By having the second unit already facing in that direction, with a clear field of view and path of travel, he can initiate immediate pursuit with the second unit following as soon as possible. This tactic will facilitate faster capture and less possibility of injury or property damage resulting from police action.

Figures 4, 5, and 6 illustrate the locations and positions described. The maximum number of units illustrated in the diagrams is two. This is not to say that roadblock locations must be limited to two units. Other units may be parked as strategically as the terrain will allow following the original pattern of the first two.

The law enforcement agencies in a county (which would include the city police departments, the sheriff's office, and the local highway patrol station) should meet and develop a county-wide roadblock plan that will provide mutual assistance to any of those jurisdictions in the event of a major crime. By taking a map of the county and marking those intersections or locations that are strategic in terms of escape from any city within the county, it is possible to develop a network that will cover most situations in which flight is taken by automobile. Each department then will be given an assignment to cover certain locations, which should be numbered. Each radio dispatch center needs a large map clearly marked showing these locations and their numbers displayed in plain view for the dispatcher.

When a crime occurs in which the roadblock plan is needed, the agency which has jurisdiction over the crime can initiate the plan by alerting the agencies by radio or telephone and request-

Felony Stops and Roadblocks 99

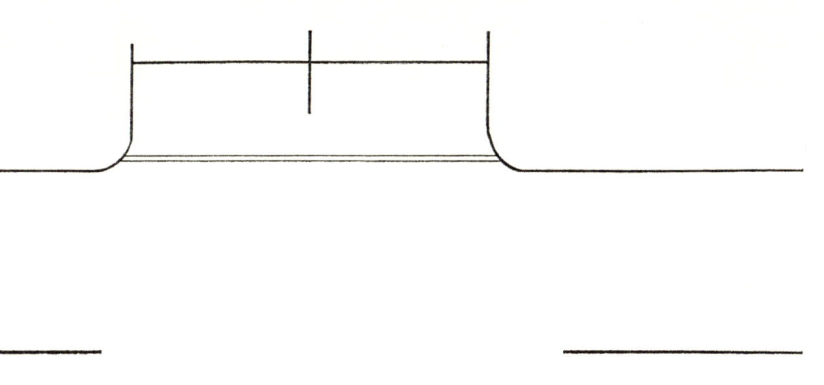

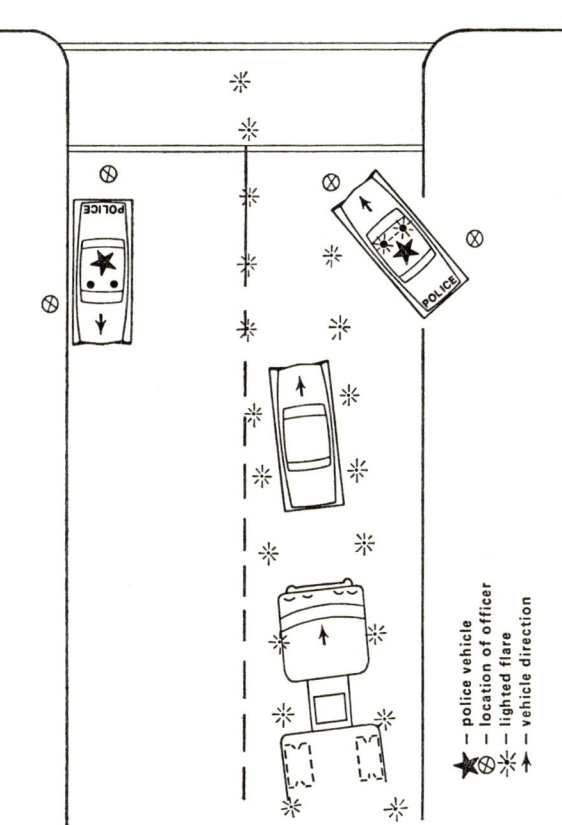

Figure 4. Roadblock position for two police units on a two-lane highway at an intersection. The flare pattern channels traffic past the primary unit for inspection. The unit across the street is facing the opposite direction for pursuit purposes.

★ — police vehicle
⊗ — location of officer
※ — lighted flare
↑ — vehicle direction

Figure 4.

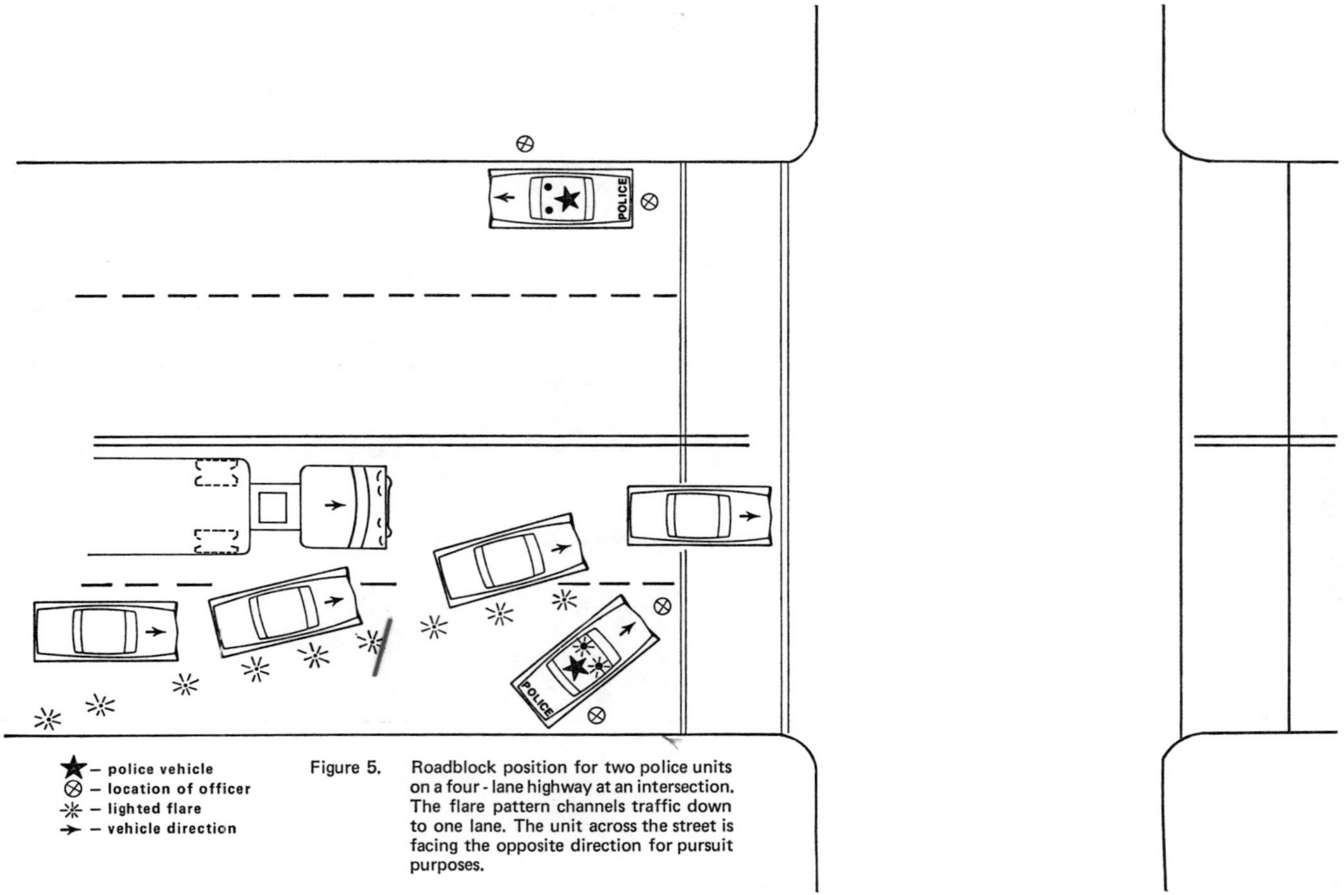

Figure 5. Roadblock position for two police units on a four-lane highway at an intersection. The flare pattern channels traffic down to one lane. The unit across the street is facing the opposite direction for pursuit purposes.

★ – police vehicle
⊗ – location of officer
✷ – lighted flare
↑ – vehicle direction

Figure 5.

Felony Stops and Roadblocks   101

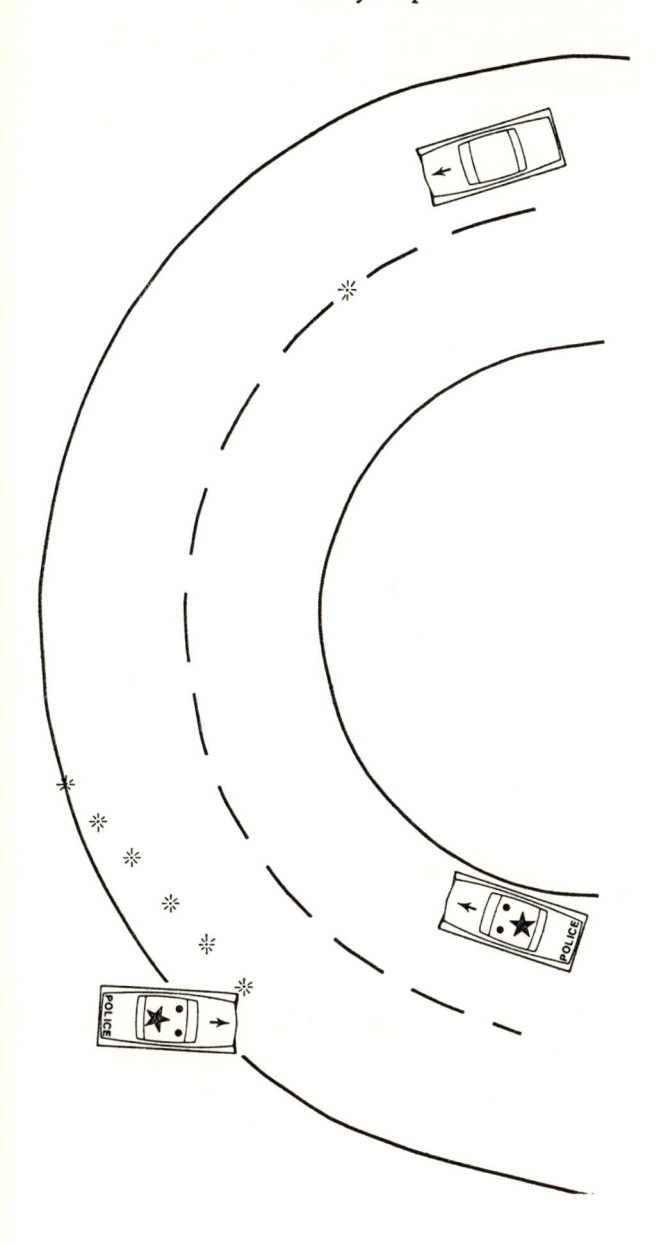

Figure 6. Roadblock position for two police units on a curve. The flare at the beginning of the curve is to warn traffic of a hazard ahead. Additional flares are used to attract attention to the primary unit and to further slow traffic. The second unit is facing the opposite direction for pursuit purposes.

★ – police vehicle
⊗ – location of officer
✶ – lighted flare
→ – vehicle direction

Figure 6.

ing immediate action on the roadblock system. In Humboldt County, which is located in northern California, such a plan has been devised and entitled, "666." When this plan is activated, the agency calling for assistance notifies the other agencies that a "666" is in effect, e.g. armed robbery at the Bank of America in Eureka, and follows with a description of the suspect vehicle and occupants. Supervisors of the other law enforcement agencies then respond by deploying their units to locations which have been assigned in advance to their agency. The units carry a card in each patrol car behind the sunvisor so that an officer who does not remember the sequence of numbered locations has a quick reference. When numbered locations are used, the possibility is eliminated of fleeing felons who have a police monitor overhearing the locations that are covered and avoiding them. What they will hear is a police dispatcher deploying a certain unit to location number five. Without the chart they will not know where that is and may very well approach that location. When the units are in place at their designated locations, the originating agency is notified by the assisting agencies, and all units stand by until further notice.

By working in concert, it is possible for law enforcement agencies to make maximum use of the total resources available in a county and greatly increase the possibility of apprehending fleeing felons.

One of the ways to improve the efficiency of agencies working together is to conduct periodic drills. The only way this can be done with realism is to keep the drill secret until it is in progress. A decoy vehicle posing as the suspects, but containing law enforcement personnel in plain clothes, will leave the imaginary location of the crime and attempt to leave the county without being stopped. When the roadblock is initiated, it should be stressed that this is a drill in order to minimize the possibility of an accidental injury because an officer believes a real crime is in progress. These drills should be performed no less than quarterly in order to keep the system working efficiently.

CHAPTER TWELVE

INTOXICATED DRIVER DETECTION

THE MATERIAL in this chapter is intended to provide the reader with the necessary information to accomplish the following:
- Understand the effect of alcohol and other drugs
- Recognize driving behavior which may indicate intoxication
- Develop the ability to recognize intoxication symptoms through the use of field sobriety tests
- Understand the difference between "under the influence" and "intoxicated."
- Recognize the difference of the effects of drugs versus alcohol and drugs in combination with alcohol
- Recognize the difference between illness and intoxication
- Recognize the alcoholic and his ability to disguise his intoxication

It will be easier for a traffic officer to detect the presence of an intoxicated driver if he understands the effects of alcohol and other drugs on the human body. If the individual officer has had some personal experience with the use of alcohol (and possibly other drugs), he will understand better the causes of behavior that he observes in the field.

Part of the drinking driver enforcement training at the California Highway Patrol Academy includes a lab period in which volunteer cadets are allowed to choose the type of liquid alcoholic refreshment that they wish, and they are monitored throughout an evening while they partake. At the end of approximately four hours of controlled drinking, they are brought before the class, one at a time, and put through a roadside sobriety test in order to demonstrate the effects of alcohol. The students are chosen because of various backgrounds in the use of alcohol. Usually, one considers himself a fairly heavy drinker with the ability to "hold his liquor." Another may consider himself to be a moderate social drinker, and at least one is a teetotaler. There will be a varied difference in the effects that alcohol will have on these types. The purpose of this lab is to provide the basic student with specific observation experience that will help him to form logical conclusions about sobriety in the field.

The use of alcohol in combination with other drugs, sometimes intentional and sometimes not, is becoming more common. In the case of a person who is taking a prescription drug and forgets the doctor's direction not to drink alcohol, the unintentional version may be found. On the other hand, the addict, whether an alcoholic or drug addict, may use the two in combination for a more emphatic effect. Alcohol may also be used to cover the intake of other drugs. When that is the case, the presence of a liquor breath is hoped to distract the officer from thinking in terms of other drugs.

Alcohol is a depressant drug. It causes the human system to slow down and, in the extreme stages, to stop. The question has been asked, "Why then, if alcohol is a depressant, do people become more active and carry on in the wild manner that many do at parties instead of slowing down and going to sleep?" The answer is that they are on their way to that final point of going to sleep; however, the relaxation effect of alcohol on the body has a tranquilizing reaction and the social inhibitions that people carry with them during their normal day are usually laid aside. Many people experience regret the following day, after recognizing their behavior while under the influence of alcohol the night before.

Since alcohol is a depressant, it has the effect of slowing down the system and interfering with the psychomotor skills, such as balance and eye-hand coordination. A person walks, talks, and moves more slowly while drinking alcohol. He also does not react as quickly to events around him. This is why it is dangerous for a person under the influence of alcohol to drive an automobile.

A person who is under the influence of alcohol and drives a car will exhibit a variety of actions which can be predicted and interpreted when observed on the highway. The individual's personality goes through a change as the effect of the alcohol becomes stronger in the system. It has already been mentioned that the inhibitions are set aside. A middle aged, conservative businessman may be found attempting to have a drag race with a teenager on the highway. The officer may see a person who is aware of his condition driving very slowly, concentrating very hard, trying to make it home.

The drinker experiences a loss of awareness while under the influence of alcohol, even though the illusion is that awareness is heightened. The loss of awareness occurs as the senses are dulled and they begin to overlook minor things in driving. One particular symptom at night is the drinking driver who fails to dim his headlights when driving in traffic. If the officer notices a car with headlights on high beam, being driven without regard to the flashing headlights of other motorists who are trying to signal, he may be observing an intoxicated driver.

A driver who goes either particularly slow or fast and who has a tendency to weave slightly or drastically may be an intoxicated driver. It seems as though the harder an intoxicated driver works at keeping the car in a straight course, the more exaggerated the weave becomes. Also, distraction with conversation or other pursuits will cause the driver not to notice that he is drifting out of his lane.

Stop signs and road signals may be seen only at the very last minute, and an intoxicated driver will either go through without realizing it or stop partially into the intersection.

Pulling alongside a person who is intoxicated, the officer may notice an intent stare indicative of the tunnel vision that occurs in the advanced stages of intoxication. The driver will grasp the steering wheel, lean forward, and stare intently at the highway, possibly without being aware of the officer's presence alongside in a marked police car.

A person may exhibit symptoms similar to intoxication, such as slurred speech, disorientation, poor balance, glassy-eyed appearance, and dilated pupils, but these may actually be the symptoms of illness rather than drinking. Diabetics will sometimes exhibit these symptoms and may even have a metallic breath which is similar to stale liquor. Unfortunately, these symptoms have been mistaken before by law enforcement officers, and people have died in the drunk tank from lack of medication. It is very important that an officer observing a person who is apparently intoxicated should delve into the possibility of illness before forming an opinion.

When talking with a suspected drunk driver at the roadside, the traffic officer needs to explore the illness aspect by asking questions about the person's welfare. These health questions will include such items as, "Are you under a doctor's care for anything?" "Have you been taking any medication?" "Have you been treated for diabetes?" or "Do you now have diabetes?" "How much sleep have you had in the last twenty-four hours?" "Have you had a head injury recently?" "Have you been to a dentist?" This line of questioning is intended to discover the possibility of illness or the use of medication that may cause symptoms of intoxication.

The field sobriety test is one means of examining the condition of a person suspected of being intoxicated. It is a series of balance and coordination exercises that are demonstrated by the officer and are intended to simulate normal activity and test psychomotor control. The tests are an additional set of facts to be considered in forming an opinion about the driver's sobriety.

FINGER-TO-NOSE. The first test is intended to determine what degree of psychomotor control the driver possesses, by touching a known point when unable to see it. The test is conducted with the suspected driver standing erect and extending the arms at the shoulders to form a standing cross. The instruction is to extend the index finger of each hand and close the eyes. Upon command, the driver is to touch the tip of the designated index finger to the tip of the nose and return the arm to the extended position.

During the tests it is appropriate for the officer to first demonstrate each test in order to more clearly establish what he wants, and also to prove that the test is possible with a minimum of effort. The exception to that rule is the finger-to-nose. The officer may demonstrate it, only he should do it with his eyes open. It does not take a great deal of imagination to see what might happen with an officer standing on the roadside, eyes closed, arms extended out, offering himself as a target for attack. People who are under the influence of alcohol and/or drugs experience personality changes which may make them far more dangerous at that moment than any other time. It is possible to demonstrate this test without closing the eyes and, therefore, not exposing oneself to attack.

A variation of the finger-to-nose begins in the same manner, only the requirement is to touch the index fingers together in front of the person's body with the eyes closed. The officer is looking for a degree of accuracy or inaccuracy in either example. If the individual successfully touches the tip of the nose with the right index finger, but finds the upper lip with the left index finger, those points need to be recorded. A variation of results will be seen throughout all the tests given; some tests will be performed successfully, others will not. All the information is relevant and should be recorded.

SIMPLE BALANCE TEST, No. 1. The simple balance test is performed by standing on one foot and raising the opposite foot slightly off the ground. When requiring this test, it should be done on level, smooth ground so that balance is not affected by a grade of unevenness of the road surface. The officer may wish to perform this test himself while the suspected driver is doing so. The two standing side by side, both raising a foot slightly off the pavement, will provide an interesting comparison. The officer, who is sober and who possesses normal coordination, will probably stand very easily on one foot having the other slightly elevated. The suspected driver, on the other hand, will probably have to touch down with the elevated foot several times in order to maintain balance. The number of times required to touch down is a relevant fact for the report. After performing this on the right foot, it should also be done with the left, and vice versa. An important question to ask prior to requiring this test is, "Do you have any physical handicap with your back, hips, legs, ankles, or feet?" This is intended to eliminate at a later time the defense that the suspect suffered from a physical handicap which prevented the standing on one foot successfully.

SIMPLE BALANCE TEST, NO. 2. It is important to observe the suspected driver's ability to stand erect and maintain his balance. He should be directed to place his feet squarely together, heels and toes aligned and touching, hands and arms at the side, head back, eyes closed. The officer should instruct him to stand in this position until told to resume normal posture. The symptoms for which the officer is looking involve the manner in which the body reacts while attempting to stand erect. Some people will manage to stand fairly still and balanced. Others will sway forward and backward or in a circle or an arc. The officer needs to estimate the approximate deviation from the vertical in terms of inches and also in terms of seconds in order to graphically describe the reaction to this test.

Again, a note of caution. It may be hazardous for the officer to demonstrate this test by standing with his head back and eyes closed in front of a suspected driver. Therefore, he can just as well verbally describe the actions required without exposing himself to danger.

WALKING HEEL-TO-TOE. The heel-to-toe demonstration is fairly well known to the public and is also commonly referred to as "walking the line." Actually a line is not necessary to complete the test; an imaginary line will suffice. However, if a painted line or a crack in the sidewalk is available and the subject wishes to use it for reference, he may do so. The purpose of this test is to measure the balance coordination and psychomotor skills as well as the ability to follow instructions.

A point to remember when giving any of the roadside sobriety tests is that following instructions is a part of the examination.

A person whose mind is fogged by alcohol or drugs will not likely perceive all instructions or comply with all instructions. This may be compared with a sober person, faced with police inquiry at the roadside, who will probably pay intense attention to the instructions and execute them perfectly, realizing the consequences if he fails.

The heel-to-toe is executed as though walking a tightrope. The heel of one foot is placed directly in front of and touching the toe of the other. The weight is then transferred to the forward foot and the rear foot brought around and placed in front, heel-to-toe, and so on.

It is important to instruct the subject in exactly how many steps to take. For example, "Walk away from me, heel-to-toe, taking *seven* *s*teps and upon the *seventh* step, pivot around and return with *seven* steps." If the subject takes more than seven steps this is to be noted as failure to follow instructions, possibly due to an alcohol-affected brain.

When the subject does pivot and turn around, his balance should be observed carefully, because a sudden spinning around by a person under the influence of liquor will usually result in a loss of balance. Again, this is an item for the officer's report.

The foregoing tests are usually sufficient, coupled with observation of driving and observation of the subject's general appearance and demeanor, to determine whether or not he is sober. However, if the student wishes additional ideas on testing the roadside sobriety, the following are several more.

PICK UP THE FLASHLIGHT. A flashlight placed in a standing position on the ground is the object of focus for the subject. He should be instructed to point to the flashlight and walk in a circle around it three times, then pick it up and hand it to the officer. If the individual is under the influence of alcohol, he will probably not be able to complete the three turns around the flashlight without staggering, and then may have some difficulty in picking the flashlight up because of dizziness. Another symptom evidenced after picking up the flashlight is that the person will be disoriented by the circling and try to hand the flashlight to an empty space rather than where the officer is actually standing. He will usually recognize his error and be seen searching visually for where the officer has gone. Some people who are fairly well intoxicated may fall down in performing this test. Caution should be used when dealing with an obviously intoxicated person. This test will usually crack the veneer of an accomplished drinker who has been able to concentrate hard enough to perform other tests fairly well. It should be reserved for the time when the officer has doubts about a person's sobriety rather than used with someone whose sobriety is no longer a question.

PICKING UP THE COIN. An officer may use the coin test to ascertain the perception ability and manual dexterity of the suspect. He should tell the suspect that he is going to place a coin on the ground and wants the suspect to pick it up and hand it back. When the suspect attempts to pick up the coin, the officer should observe any difficulty the suspect may have in getting his fingers to work properly to pry the coin away from the pavement. When the suspect hands the coin to the officer, the officer should put it in his pocket and ask what denomination it was (a quarter, a nickel, etc.). If the suspect is able to answer correctly, the officer should ask whether the coin was heads or tails while it was on the ground. This again delves into his ability to perceive things as he sees them.

COUNTING ON THE FINGERS. This test can be very useful in examining the psychomotor and manual dexterity skills of a suspected intoxicated driver who has a physical handicap or injury which prevents standing balance and coordination tests. It can also be used as an additional test.

The officer extends his hand toward the suspect and counts on the fingers, using the thumb as a counter, by saying "one, two, three, four," and going from index finger to little finger. He then hesitates at the little finger briefly and returns down the scale, "four, three, two, one." The mental powers or concentration would not normally be taxed in such a simple endeavor. However, the officer will note that the powers of concentration are severely taxed in the case of some intoxicated people. They will lose track of which finger they are counting; they will forget the number they have just said; they will find it difficult to reverse the order. The officer will even notice, in some cases, that the thumb will miss the finger. This test is a good tie breaker when the subject has done fairly well on the other standing tests.

ORAL DEXTERITY. The influence of alcohol and drugs on the speech skills of an intoxicated person is a fairly common effect. People who are "drunk" are epitimized by comedians as speaking in a very slurred, distorted manner. This occurs in varying degrees, depending on the state of intoxication. This area of bodily control may be tested during normal conversation with the suspected driver, listening for slurred speech, and documenting it in the report. The officer may not be able to recall exactly what words were slurred and how they were said unless this test is used with specific words and the results are documented.

The suspected driver should be asked to repeat several common English words after the officer. Some of the words which can be used are, *officer, electricity, methodist, episcopal,* and *aluminum.* These are words which require speech dexterity and yet are fairly common in the vocabulary of most people. These particular words also tend to exaggerate any difficulty the individual has in speaking clearly.

GENERAL OBSERVATION. While speaking with a suspected driver at the roadside, the officer needs to take in all aspects of the person's appearance. This includes such things as whether the clothing was disarranged, any urination or defecation, the hair, whether it is mussed or straight, redness of the eyes, general manner and demeanor such as flamboyant gesturing, a tendency to lean against support rather than stand erect, etc.

Special attention should be directed to the eyes of the subject. This is not only for observing the redness that is attendant to intoxication, but also pupil size. A person who is intoxicated from alcohol and a number of other drugs will have dilated pupils. The pupils and their reaction to light need to be examined. If the pupils are dilated, the officer should cover one with his hand, shine the flashlight on the back of the hand, and then remove the hand so the light shines directly into the eye. When this is done, the reaction time it takes for the pupil to constrict against the light should be carefully observed. In the case of an extremely intoxicated person, there may be almost no perceptible change. Varying degrees of intoxication will cause a slow reaction to the light. One way to compare this with a normal pupil reaction is to use a partner as a comparison. The officer can perform the same test and notice how quickly the pupils change by closing the iris against the flashlight beam. He can go back again and check the suspected driver and his partner until he is able to recall the exact comparison. If he notices that during darkness the pupils of the suspected driver are constricted, rather than dilated, it is probable that drugs, other than alcohol, are responsible.

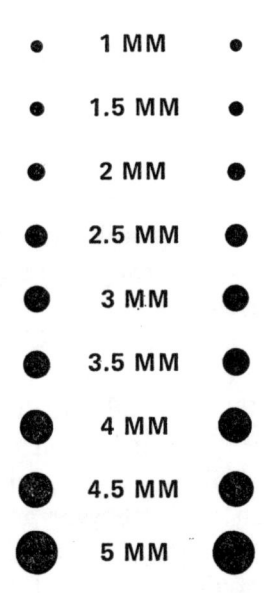

• 1 MM •

• 1.5 MM •

• 2 MM •

• 2.5 MM •

• 3 MM •

• 3.5 MM •

• 4 MM •

• 4.5 MM •

• 5 MM •

Figure 7. Examples of pupil size measurement.

At the end of this chapter is a list of some common drugs encountered on the street and some of the physical symptoms which accompany their use. By learning to recognize symptoms, the officer may be successful in determining what drug is being used and more successfully test for its presence and quantity.

The reader may have noted that throughout the chapter the

term *suspected driver* is used frequently. The purpose of this reference is to suggest that the officer withhold his opinion as to the driver's sobriety until he has accumulated considerable data. Earlier it was mentioned that some forms of illness will simulate symptoms of intoxication. Also, there are people who are sleepy and, based on a deep level of fatigue, will appear to be intoxicated. This sometimes is enhanced by one or two drinks, but would not constitute intoxication in the usual sense. It is important that the officer avoid jumping to conclusions so that he may remain objective and do a thorough job in protecting the rights of the suspected driver as well.

The alcoholic is a person who is addicted to the drug alcohol. Alcoholism is far more prevalent than many would suspect. A person who is addicted to the use of alcohol requires its presence in his system throughout the day in order to appear and behave in a normal manner. The level of alcohol in the blood stream required to produce a "normal appearance" varies with the degree of addiction. There are people who need more than the legal limit required to be presumed intoxicated in many states just to feel normal. Consequently, these people live with alcohol always and are able to deceive their friends, loved ones, business associates, and others by acting sober while actually being under the influence of alcohol.

When alcoholics drive a car or do other activities, not in the presence of others, they tend to relax and may show some symptoms of intoxication. These symptoms may show up in the driving and draw the officer's attention. However, when the person exits from the vehicle he reassumes the role he plays in his everyday life and will meet the officer with the appearance of one who is sober and totally in control of himself. The officer may be talking with a person who is considerably under the influence of alcohol, but will not be able to tell at first glance. Many officers with short experience in observing intoxicated persons have released people who are alcoholics, thinking that they were not under the influence.

It will require considerable concentration and study on the officer's part in order to recognize subtle subjective symptoms which will escape the untrained eye. While an alcoholic is being observed and scrutinized, he will usually continue the charade and do so successfully, especially if it means the possible loss of his livelihood in being arrested. It is only when he relaxes that he slips up. When dealing with a person who may be in this category, the officer will have better success if he relaxes the individual by appearing not to be concerned about the possibility of intoxication. Talk of other things in a comfortable, light manner will tend to relax the person and lull him into a sense of security. When this occurs, very small slips will be made. The officer may not be able to detect them unless he's very watchful. If he sees a momentary balance problem, slight slurring of the speech, wandering of the attention, or an increase in agitated behavior, these may indicate a higher level of intoxication than is otherwise apparent.

It is suggested that the traffic officer spend as much time as possible studying the objective and subjective symptoms displayed by persons in various stages of intoxication. This will increase his ability to accurately diagnose what he is seeing at the roadside. It will also assure a higher degree of accuracy in making arrests.

Common Drugs Encountered on the Street

AMPHETAMINE — This drug is also known on the street as "speed." It is a stimulant. It has various names depending on the manufacturer. It causes hyperactive behavior. The pulse rate is very rapid. People who are under the influence of amphetamines will react drastically to situations, sometimes with panic, other times with extreme anger or fear. Amphetamines when combined with alcohol produce a confusing set of symptoms. The user will demonstrate erractic behavior which may be the result of the contradictory effects of a stimulant versus a depressant. The pupils of the eye will be dilated. When combined with alcohol, a synergistic effect may occur.

BARBITURATES — A depressant drug. Pupils of the eyes may

be constricted. Overdose will cause dilation, impaired judgement, slurred speech, loss of coordination, similar to alcohol. When combined with alcohol, a synergistic effect may occur.

COCAINE — Powder form, usually sniffed into the nostrils. Causes excitement, alternating with periods of depression. Sometimes produces violent behavior due to release of inhibitions. Excessive use may cause hallucinations, tremors, paranoia, etc.

HASHISH — Concentrated derivative of marijuana. Obtained from the marijuana plants by means of removing surface resin which contains high concentration of tetrahydrocanabonal (THC). Similar symptoms with marijuana, only magnified. Inflammation of the eyes, dilation of the pupils. Behavior varies from talkative, active, jovial, to euphoric or drowsy. Distortion of time, distance, and speed occurs.

LYSERGIC ACID DIETHYLAMIDE (LSD) — Hallucinogenic chemical which produces visual and auditory fantasy in varying degrees. Pupilary dilation. No other constant physical symptom. User experiences difficulty in differentiating between fantasy and reality. No available chemical test to measure the amount in the blood stream. Difficult to determine its presence. Subjects exhibiting eccentric behavior may be under the influence of LSD.

MARIJUANA — Odor similar to burnt alfalfa on the clothing and in the hair and on the breath. Subject who is intoxicated with marijuana will be disoriented as to distance, time, and speed. May drive a vehicle at a high rate of speed and be convinced that he is driving very slowly or vice versa. Redness of the eyes, dilated pupils. No known chemical tests for determining amount in the blood stream. If it is necessary to prove the use of marijuana, the clothing may be removed and processed for evidence, a comb run through the hair, beard, etc. Cotton swab circulated through the interior of the mouth collecting saliva will show traces of marijuana presence.

OPIATE DERIVATIVES — (MORPHINE, HEROIN, ETC.)
Symptoms include lack of coordination, lethargic movements, drowsiness, reduced respiration, sleepy appearance. During withdrawals subject exhibits restlessness, increase in respiration and blood pressure, experiences cramps, muscle spasm, nausea, diarrhea, etc. Determination of opiate presence requires nalline test or urinalysis.

CHAPTER THIRTEEN

INTOXICATED DRIVER ARREST PROCEDURE

THE MATERIAL in this chapter is intended to provide the reader with the necessary information to accomplish the following:
- Safely confine an intoxicated driver upon arrest
- Determine what to do with passengers
- Protect the arrested driver's vehicle and its contents
- Use chemical tests to prove intoxication
- Use tape recordings and videotapes to prove intoxication

When a traffic officer arrests an intoxicated driver, he is dealing with a person whose personality has been altered chemically by the ingestion of alcohol and possibly other drugs. It is also the case that the person's physical coordination is impaired. For both reasons it is important that the officer safely confine the intoxicated driver once the arrest is made.

A person whose personality is altered by alcohol is not predictable, and it is unsafe to trust the individual to remain unconfined. This means that handcuffs should be used when arresting an intoxicated driver. Some officers will argue this point and state that they have arrested many drunk drivers without the need to use handcuffs. They will be quick to point out that by soliciting the cooperation of the arrestee in exchange for not using handcuffs, they have found the arrest procedure to be very compatible. This may be the case for some, but there are those individuals who become dangerous when intoxicated and will not always telegraph in advance the potential hazard that they present. It was mentioned in an earlier chapter that the confirmed alcoholic becomes very crafty in concealing his condition. This same individual also has the ability to conceal his intent to attempt escape or to attack the officer.

If a person is not capable of managing his vehicle in traffic due to an altered condition of mind and body, he is not responsible enough to trust in an arrest situation. Several times during my career I have been aware of tragic circumstances which have been the result of an intoxicated driver who was arrested, but not handcuffed. The driver, on some occasions, attacked the officer during transit, which meant the officer had to attempt to defend himself while trying to control his automobile in traffic. In some other cases, officers have been killed under these circumstances, quite often with their own sidearms, or with a weapon which was concealed upon the person of the arrestee.

Another tragic situation is the case of the intoxicated driver who does not offer physical resistance but attempts to flee and is run down by traffic and killed, or who attempts to get out of the patrol car while it is traveling down the highway toward the jail. Not only is this unfortunate for the person who dies, but it is also difficult for the officer to justify why he did not take proper security procedures to prevent it.

It is possible for an officer to diplomatically notify an arrested driver that it is normal procedure for all persons arrested to be handcuffed, for their own safety as well as the officer's. Not all of them will willingly agree, but the prudent officer will persist and require handcuffs to be worn.

It is further necessary, while transporting in the patrol vehicle, to insist that a seat belt be worn by the arrestee. Should the patrol vehicle be involved in a traffic accident en route to the jail facility, and the arrestee is handcuffed behind his back but not wearing a seat belt, he will be a helpless victim. He has absolutely no way to defend against an impact with the windshield or other parts of the vehicle. If the seat belt is properly applied, it will also serve as an additional restraint in order to confine the arrestee to one location in the vehicle.

If the patrol vehicle has a cage section, it is recommended that the arrested driver be located in the right rear seat and a seat belt attached. This method provides the officer with a quick glance over his shoulder as sufficient means of keeping track of his subject. If the patrol vehicle is not equipped with a security partition, then the arrested party should be placed in the right front seat, handcuffed, and seat belt fastened. The officer may apply additional control to the subject while en route by inserting his baton through the left elbow of the subject from the back side with the far end of the baton extending into the groin area. By holding onto the butt end of the baton with his right hand, the officer can exert pressure to turn the subject away from him and simultaneously apply pressure to the groin, which will encourage the subject to desist should he attempt to spit on the officer or engage in more violent conduct.

When an intoxicated driver is arrested and he is accompanied by passengers, the officer must decide what to do with them. If they are not intoxicated also, he can release them. The arrestee may wish to release his vehicle to one of the members of the party, but the officer should use caution in this regard. Later, when sober, the driver may not recall giving permission for the vehicle to be released. He may not, in fact, be capable of making a rational decision during his intoxicated state. Therefore, if the officer decides to allow the release to the second party, he should carefully document the identity of the person and examine his driver's license and other identification to verify where he may be reached at a later time.

If passengers in the arrested party's vehicle are intoxicated, but not to a degree that they cannot care for their own safety, it may be appropriate to call a taxi for their further transportation from the scene. Depending on local regulations, it would not normally be necessary to arrest the passengers, unless there is no other way to facilitate their departure. If the passengers are intoxicated to a point that they are unable to care for themselves or if they become a problem due to their conduct, arrest may be the only solution.

Sometimes taking a few extra minutes to call a friend who will come and transport them home will save the officer time in the long run, which he would have to spend in booking the additional persons.

Once the intoxicated driver has been arrested and confined in the patrol vehicle, the officer's next responsibility is the arrested driver's vehicle and its contents. Since the officer's duty is to protect life and property, and further, since he has removed the driver from his vehicle, he must take reasonable steps to insure its safekeeping. This can be simply done in many cases by examining the contents in plain view in the vehicle to determine if anything of value needs further securement. Once this is done, the vehicle may be locked and left parked at its location, if it is in a legal parking area. If it has been established in the courts that once an officer has made a reasonable effort to secure the property, it is no longer his responsibility if the vehicle is stolen or vandalized. It would be no different than if the driver himself had parked the vehicle in that location under normal circumstances and was victimized. The officer is not responsible for the arrested driver's property beyond the reasonable care requirement because the arrested driver has willfully placed himself in the position of being arrested by his self-inflicted intoxication. Therefore, the responsibility of the vehicle is truly his own.

In some areas officers are required to store the vehicle and its contents with a public garage for safekeeping during the period that the owner is confined in the jail. This is done at the owner's expense. When the vehicle is stored, it is necessary to make an inventory of those items which are in plain view in order to insure their return to the owner. It is neither legal nor justified for an officer to use the storage inventory procedure as a ruse to search the vehicle for evidence that may be used to prosecute additional crimes. The officer already has the right to search the vehicle incidental to the arrest for drunk driving. He may search for the instrumentalities of the crime which, in this case, would be additional containers of alcohol and possibly drugs. Since he is permitted to search for contraband related to the arrest, he may conduct a reasonable perusal of the vehicle's contents. It is not reasonable that this inquiry extend into a locked trunk or involve the opening of locked suitcases, sealed packages, etc. None of these areas would contain either liquor or drugs available to the driver while operating his vehicle. If a closed suitcase is in the vehicle, it should be inventoried as a "closed suitcase, blue in color, etc."

The arrested driver should be asked if he has anything of unusual value in his vehicle that needs to be secured. Some people carry large quantities of cash in their car. It may be found stashed under floor mats, behind seats, in the glove compartment, etc. If the individual has the cash in the vehicle, he will probably want it with him at the jail. When the officer is told of an item of value or of cash in the vehicle, he should go directly to the location and retrieve it. Cash should be counted carefully in the presence of the driver and then placed in his own pocket. When he arrives at the jail, it will be removed and placed in his property and he will receive a receipt. The officer should not place it in his pocket to hold for the driver until arrival at the jail. This procedure allows too much opportunity for forgetting that it is there, or for a discrepancy on the amount upon arrival. If the officer has a partner or if there are witnesses present, it would be very useful to count out the money in their presence and document their names for future protection in the event that the sobered-up driver thinks he has been robbed.

If the officer's department does not require a mandatory impound of the vehicle, then he should consider the alternative of leaving it parked and locked at the scene, if that is possible. If the vehicle is stopped out in the roadway so that it would be hazardous to leave it at that location, the officer or his partner may drive it a short distance to the curb in order to leave it legally parked. The arrested driver should not be allowed to move his own vehicle. Once he has been arrested it would not be appropriate to allow this intoxicated driver to again get behind the wheel. His behavior is unpredictable; he might just drive away and leave the officer standing in the roadway. Should this occur, and he becomes involved in a traffic accident, the officer may find himself the defendant in a lawsuit. If the vehicle will not start and the patrol car is equipped with a push bumper, the officer and his partner may push the vehicle to the curb and lock it.

It would be wise to avoid parking the vehicle on private property adjacent to the roadway without the permission of the property owner. If the arrest is made at night, it might seem wise at the time to remove the vehicle from the street by parking it in a merchant's parking lot. However, the following business day, the merchant may not agree with the decision and have the vehicle towed away himself. If there is any difficulty with leaving the vehicle parked and locked, if there is any doubt in the officer's mind as to the safety of the location, or if the vehicle is not able to be secured due to defective windows, locks, etc., then a storage for safekeeping would be the best alternative.

The next step in the arrest procedure is to obtain physical evidence to support the officer's opinion that the arrested driver is intoxicated. This may be done by obtaining one or more chemical tests to determine the blood/alcohol level of the subject. The local district attorney will have stated what guidelines he wishes to be followed in drinking driver arrests. His wishes should be considered since his officer will be prosecuting the case. If the district attorney prefers a blood test, every effort should be made to obtain one. The United States Supreme Court has ruled that officers have the right to secure physical evidence when making an arrest for crime. They have specifically designated body fluids in this category. If it is necessary to obtain a sample of an arrested person's blood to prove his intoxication and the sample is taken in a medically approved manner, the procedure would be considered appropriate. Any force that might be necessary to obtain a blood sample must be governed by the policy of the department as well as by the law in the area. It is the general policy of most departments not to use force to obtain a blood sample in a misdemeanor drunk driving case. The use of force probably will not be necessary if the officer will use tact and persuasiveness in his dealing with the arrested driver. Many arrested drivers will reconcile themselves to the inevitability of a blood sample being taken and will not resist the process. Others will not cooperate with anything the officer tries and he may as well give up on the blood sample with them.

Other chemical tests include breath samples and urinalysis. In the case of breath samples, a number of devices are available for use. They include the Breathalyzer, the Intoxalyzer, and others. The main principles involved in testing a breath sample for blood/alcohol level is based on a color change of certain chemicals when injected with the breath sample. The rate of color change and the amount of color change are measured to determine a precalibrated level which is comparable to a blood/alcohol level. Unless the officer is specifically trained in the use of these devices, it would be better to obtain the services of a laboratory technologist or other specialist who can properly secure the sample, test it, and testify to the results in court.

A urinalysis is useful in determining blood/alcohol level. It is also useful in searching for traces of other drugs that may be in the system. It is possible to obtain more information on some drugs through urinalysis than through a blood sample. The subject should be required to void his bladder, and a sample should be taken of the voiding as well as a second sample within approximately twenty minutes or one-half hour. It is the second sample which is tested for blood/alcohol level, as well as drug presence. The first sample is only proof of the voiding of the bladder, which is recommended procedure.

Reasonable privacy while a urine sample is given must be assured. This does not mean that the security of the sample must be compromised. The officer may be present while the subject produces the urine specimen, but should remove him to a restroom area where he is out of the view of others. If the arrested driver is a female, then a jail matron should handle the procedure.

One benefit of a breath analysis is that instant results are available. If an obviously intoxicated subject is in custody, but a breath analysis indicates very little alcohol in the bloodstream, it is a sure sign that other chemical agents are present, and an effort should be made to take either a blood or urine specimen to screen for drug level presence.

In the case of a manslaughter or serious felony, it may be

necessary to use force to obtain body fluids for evidence. It is very dangerous to insert a needle into the vein of a person who is struggling physically at the time. The needle may break and be carried away into an artery or the heart, which will very likely be fatal to the subject. Even with several burly policemen holding the subject down, it will still be dangerous to attempt removal of a blood sample under these circumstances. If the subject is physically resisting to the point that the procedure will be dangerous, it is recommended that an officer who is familiar with the carotid choke apply it on the subject, rendering him unconscious long enough to withdraw the blood sample. This will be for the subject's own safety and will also avoid unnecessary struggle, torn uniforms, and possible injury to the officers.

Other evidence of an intoxicated driver's condition may include tape recordings and videotapes or movies. It is practical for a traffic officer to carry a tape recorder with him on duty. He may turn the tape recorder on at any time during the roadside contact depending on its portability. If the tape recorder is not adequately portable to use out of the car, it may be started when the interrogation begins in the patrol car. It is not necessary to notify the subject of the presence of a tape recorder. He is not entitled to expect privacy in the interior of a police car while in custody. The recording will also include the officer's own voice as a party of the conversation, and this involvement entitles him further to use the tape in court. A tape recording of the voice of an intoxicated person is appropriate evidence of that person's lack of sobriety. The person will be loud and possibly vulgar in his language, which differs from his normal conduct. He will often make wild, radical statements and generally behave in a raucous manner which will convince most juries, in a quiet courtroom, of his true, condition at the time. Quite often a defense attorney, upon hearing the tape recording taken at the scene, will recommend that his client change his plea rather than risk the verdict in court against such evidence.

If the arrested driver refuses to submit to a chemical test of his blood, breath, or urine, it will be helpful for the officer to have the additional evidence of a tape recording to add to his own testimony. Some jail facilities are equipped with movie cameras or videotape recorders. These devices are exceptionally useful in capturing the true condition of the intoxicated driver at the time of arrest. Such a record of the event will allow a jury to be transported backward in time to the night of the arrest and observe what may be a very comical, disheveled, and obviously intoxicated clown. When this is compared with the conservative dress and manner of the defendant in the courtroom, it will be very damaging evidence, indeed.

The procedure in some locations where videotapes or movies are taken at the jail includes a reenactment of the roadside balance tests. Sometimes, the passage of time between the roadside arrest and arrival at the jail will allow the arrested driver to absorb even more alcohol into his system. If he has just left a bar prior to arrest, there will be undigested alcohol in his stomach. The time it takes, depending on distance, to travel to the jail will allow some of this alcohol to be digested into the system, and further the effect on the subject's coordination and balance.

It is important in any criminal case for the officer to take advantage of all evidence that is available. To fail to do so is a form of laziness or lack of knowledge. He may not need all of the evidence to convict the subject, but he does have it if needed. Everything available, including chemical tests, tape recordings, videotapes, or movies, should be used to bring the real story of what happened that night before the jury so that justice will have its day in court.

CHAPTER FOURTEEN

INTOXICATED DRIVER ARREST REPORTS

THE MATERIAL in this chapter is intended to provide the reader with the necessary information to accomplish the following:

* Properly document the identity of the person arrested
* Properly document the description and ownership information for the vehicle used by the intoxicated driver
* Complete the remaining general information necessary for DWI report
* Organize the narrative by the use of major headings.

The first consideration for an arrest report is to properly record the identity of the person arrested. Most police reports adequately provide blanks for the data necessary; jurisdictions vary, but some states require criminal identification data for state records. Primarily, the officer is interested in making sure that he has adequately identified the person in custody. False identification is fairly prevalent, and police officers must be constantly mindful of this possibility. The arrested person will, of course, be photographed and fingerprinted at the jail. However, if he is released on bail prior to verification of the fingerprints, it may be too late.

The beginning portion of an arrest report should contain areas for the name, address, race, sex, date of birth, color of hair and eyes, height, and weight. There is some quarrel with the need for recording the race of the subject. Race is a fact and may be relevant in determining identity. Given a warrant for

John M. Jones, described as being thirty-five years of age, 6 feet tall, 180 pounds, with black hair and brown eyes, it is not known if the person is a fair Caucasian, swarthy-complexioned European, or a person with African ancestry. The issue must be dealt with by policy.

After the preliminary identity has been recorded, supplemental identification information should also be recorded. This would include the driver's license number, social security number, place of birth, employment information, and any numbers which are on file for this subject from previous bookings.

If the arrested person has no identification documents in his possession, other steps must be taken to verify identity. Once in a while a person will leave home without taking his wallet, which contains his personal identification papers. An officer can sometimes verify the identity of a person who apparently "matches" the vehicle by asking questions about the contents of the glove compartment. Sometimes there will be credit card slips or other identifying documents which the subject can describe. Perhaps there will be a document having a signature that can be compared with the one of the arrested party.

If none of the above are successful, then every effort should be made to detain the subject at the jail until his fingerprints have been processed with the FBI or state officials to determine the identity. Some motor vehicle departments use fingerprints as part of their records. This may be a quick way to verify identity.

The vehicle information will be as important as the person. Careful documentation of the vehicle description will serve the officer in court or haunt him if it is not adequate. Usually a court appearance is many months removed from the evening of the arrest, and the memory tends to fade during passage of time. Therefore, it is important to have complete records to refer to when testifying. The license number, state from which it was issued, and the year it was issued are preliminary and basic items that are needed. It is also important to describe the vehicle by year, make, body style, and color. As has been stated in earlier chapters, the true verification of the vehicle's identity is not in the license plate but in the VIN. That number must be located and recorded on the arrest report. It is important to verify the ownership of the vehicle by checking both the VIN and license numbers with DMV and the Department of Justice to determine ownership and status.

The disposition of a vehicle is important especially to the driver when he is released. The report should indicate whether the vehicle was stolen or left at the scene. In the case of the few times that a vehicle may be released to a second party, with the owner's consent, careful documentation of who that person was, is an important part of the report.

When a drunk driving arrest takes place, there will occasionally be witnesses who will be important to record. Sometimes there will be passengers in the vehicle; at other times there will be bystanders. It is important to obtain an adequate amount of information about a witness in order to facilitate a follow-up contact at a later date. This would include the witness's name, address, sex, and age, as well as a residence telephone number and, if possible, a business telephone number. If a witness is listed on the face of an arrest report, the body or narrative section should include a brief synopsis of what he observed and to what he will testify.

The fact that the arrested party was properly advised of his rights should necessarily be documented and easily located on the face of the report. A basic description of the words used to admonish the subject, along with the time and the name of the officer who made the statement, should be included. Additionally, clear-cut statements relating to the individual's understanding of what he has been told in reference to his rights should also be recorded. These include whether he understands the rights as explained, whether having those rights in mind he wishes to speak to the officers, and, if he agrees to speak, what type of waiver statement he has made that clearly establishes his intent to talk. This could be done briefly by recording, "Yes, I will talk with you," or "I have nothing to hide," etc. Some reference is needed to help the officer recall later the specific way in which the subject waived his right to silence.

Previously, a specific line of questioning involving the health and medical history of the subject was discussed. It is essential to document this information in order to substantiate an arrest for intoxication. Questions about the subject's health and medical background are made for the subject's benefit. It is the purpose of such questioning to determine any health hazard or medical reason why the subject would be appearing intoxicated when, in fact, he was ill or in need of medication. These questions are properly asked prior to any arrest or even prior to any roadside coordination test. Therefore, the questions do not become incriminating and may be asked prior to making the subject aware of his rights to remain silent. Health questions and other medical elimination information are documented on some reports by standard boxes which may be checked or filled in.

Other details of the field sobriety tests for alcohol or drugs include observations of the subject, and it is helpful if the report has a specific area for recording such items. If there is an odor of alcoholic beverage on the breath, the degree of odor is appropriate information — strong, moderate, or weak would be sufficient. Whether or not the subject was wearing glasses or contact lenses is an area to record and recall. Others include general attitude, appearance of the eyes, the speech, description and condition of the clothing, description of the test location, surface, weather, and lighting. It will be very important to record the latter because of the tendency on the part of some defense attorneys to blame the subject's difficulty with the tests on the location. However, if the location is described as being smooth, level, and dry, with adequate lighting either natural or artificial, this tendency will be dispelled.

A thorough defense attorney will examine every single detail of an officer's report looking for discrepancies or areas that are incomplete and may be challenged. The attorney will recognize that many officers depend on their report rather than field notes to support their memory on the witness stand. If the report is sketchy or stereotyped, it will be difficult for the officer to remember specific details of the time of arrest. The question of weather is one which may plague the officer if he does not record it. For instance, if the arrest occurred during the winter it may not be possible for the officer to recall six months later if it were raining on that specific date, or overcast, clear, etc. The attorney, on the other hand, may have researched the Weather Bureau files to find exactly what the weather was and ask the officer on the stand, especially if it is not recorded on the report. If the officer cannot remember whether or not it was raining that night, how can he be trusted to testify to the sophisticated details of a person's sobriety, etc.?

The type of tests executed at the scene of the arrest should be described in fair detail so that the way in which the test was conducted is clear to the reader of the report. If the subject was required to walk heel-to-toe in a straight line, a diagram should be included showing the pattern of steps as they were executed.

If the jurisdiction has an implied consent law which requires drivers to submit to the chemical test of their blood/alcohol level, it is appropriate and useful to have recorded on the report a statement which notifies the arrested party of this requirement, the date and time it was read, and what his response was. Any evidence that was obtained incidental to this section should be recorded as to what type of evidence, time it was taken, results if available, and disposition of any samples. The location where the test was conducted and the name and title of the person giving the test or taking the sample are all very important items.

The most difficult part of any police report for many officers is the narrative portion. There are no longer any guides or check boxes to assist him in organizing his thoughts when he reaches that point. Therefore, it is important to develop a pattern that will be complete and yet avoid the stereotyped statements. If a defense attorney subpoenas copies of previous drunk driving arrest reports of a traffic officer and, by reading some of the narrative aloud in court, establishes a stereotyped pattern of language that was used in each report, he may possibly challenge the credibility of the officer with the jury. It will sound as if "all drunks look alike" when hearing the same words used to describe each arrest. Therefore, it is important for the officer to be specific and aware of any part of the circumstances of each case that are unique. Of course there will be similarities between intoxicated persons. However, a report must have enough freedom of style and spontaneity to convince the reader that it is valid information given about a specific event and a specific person.

The formula which the author recommends for organizing the narrative of a drunk driving arrest report is very simple. It separates three main factors of the arrest procedure so that the reader can locate any piece of information quickly without having to read the entire report. It also will establish guidelines for the legality of the arrest if the officer follows this pattern in his thinking while at the roadside.

The formula referred to is PC × 3. The PC stands for Probable Cause. There are three main areas of probable cause which are involved in each drunk driving arrest. They are Probable Cause to Stop, Probable Cause to Arrest, and Probable Cause to Search.

PROBABLE CAUSE TO STOP. The actions of a drinking driver which attracted the officer's attention in the first place will be part of the probable cause to make the stop. It may be that an officer stops a vehicle because of a defective taillight or other equipment problem without being aware of the driver's condition. When he discovers the symptoms of intoxication after the stop, he then proceeds with the arrest procedure.

The original reason for stopping, if other than erratic driving, should carefully be documented as probable cause to stop. If it was due to an equipment defect on the vehicle, a citation separate from the drunk driving arrest should be issued to clearly validate that reason for stopping the vehicle. Some officers will tend to overlook the original minor equipment defect for the more serious arrest. This is a mistake because the defense may very well create a doubt in the mind of the jury as to the reason for the stop. If there is no enforcement document to support the contention that the vehicle had an equipment defect, the defense attorney can sometimes convincingly ask if it is not true that the officer stopped the vehicle on a hunch or because he knows the driver and does not like him, etc. The absence of an enforcement document will possibly add credibility to his questioning, especially if the defense presents a mechanic to testify that the vehicle in question is in perfect mechanical condition.

If erratic driving was part of the reason for the stop, it should be carefully described in the area of probable cause so that the reader can easily understand why the stop was made based on what the officer observed.

PROBABLE CAUSE TO ARREST. The previous information on why the vehicle was stopped would not be sufficient in itself for justifying an arrest on a drunk driving charge. Therefore, further information is required for the reader to understand why the officer decided to arrest the driver. This is the area where the officer's observation of the driver's driving behavior, his general appearance and demeanor out of his vehicle, the odor of liquor on his breath, his slurred speech, red eyes, failure to properly perform a sobriety test, etc., all together formed in the officer's mind the opinion that the person was intoxicated. It is very important that the officer specifically say that he did form this opinion. If he has an entry under PC to Arrest such as, "Based on the above observations, I formed the opinion that driver, Smith, was under the influence of alcohol and possibly a combination of alcohol and drugs. Therefore, I placed him under arrest," the PC to Arrest category should sum up the total observations into a neat package pointing directly toward the reasonable conclusion that the driver is intoxicated. This allows the reader to come to the same conclusion as the officer when he has the opportunity to review the same facts.

PROBABLE CAUSE TO SEARCH. The degree of search will vary with the situation. The officer should make a visual search of the interior of the arrested driver's vehicle for any evidence such as open liquor bottles, pills, marijuana cigarettes, or other contraband related to the arrest. Seizure of these items will reenforce the allegation that the driver was using intoxicants. The officer may wish to pursue a further search if he finds any of these items in plain view. That would include the glove compartment, under the seats, and any other areas within the passenger compartment to which the driver had easy access. If the officer searches the trunk of the vehicle, or any locked compartments in the vehicle, he needs to specifically state his justification and authority for the search. If he can do so legally, incidental to the arrest, he needs to outline the progression leading to the legal requirement for such a search.

A search of the arrested driver's person may be conducted, and should be conducted for the discovery of any weapons that might be turned on the officer during the trip to the jail or in the jail facilities. This is often described as a "field frisk" or "pat down." The officer also has the authority to seek any contraband related to the arrest that may be in the person's clothing. Containers of alcohol, pill boxes, marijuana cigarettes, or other drug paraphernalia would be included. Whether or not any contraband is found, it is important to document that the search was made, even with negative results.

The removal of body fluids from the arrested driver for use as physical evidence constitutes a form of search. When the officer instructs a lab technician or physician to withdraw a blood sample from the body of the arrested driver, he is searching that party's body for evidence. Therefore, the search must be justified accordingly. It is simple to state in the PC to Search category a short statement such as, "Blood sample obtained from subject, Smith, by lab tech, Johnson, at this officer's direction. Purpose of the withdrawal of blood sample is to obtain the alcohol level as evidence in prosecution of this case. Sample taken at the St. Joseph's Hospital incidental to the arrest, etc."

The division of the narrative into three major categories, Probable Cause to Stop, Probable Cause to Arrest, and Probable Cause to Search, outlines each complete piece of information which will stand the test of future inquiry by persons who have no previous knowledge of the event. They describe the legal justification for the actions of the officer described in the report. They further justify his actions in searching and seizing property belonging to the arrested subject.

It is a part of the officer's duty to prosecute successfully a criminal act committed in his presence. He is the representative of the people, and when he loses a case in court because of sloppy report writing or inadequate information, he is doing a disservice to his community. Unfortunately, some officers have a difficult time writing reports. It is hoped that the formula offered herein for the narrative portion, as well as the other parts of the intoxicated driver arrest report, will assist in eliminating this problem.

Report writing is the ribbon that binds up the package. It makes the total arrest procedure meaningful and justified. It requires a thinking person to successfully perform the duties of a police officer in our society. Consider this carefully when deciding whether to enter this field of employment. If the reader is already involved in police work he must focus a great deal of attention and effort on this part of his duties and improve it constantly.

CHAPTER FIFTEEN

COURT TESTIMONY

THE MATERIAL in this chapter is intended to provide the reader with the necessary information to accomplish the following:

- Present an acceptable appearance in court
- Prepare complete testimony by reviewing notes, reports, and previous transcripts
- Avoid emotional response to attorneys who attempt to discredit or discount testimony
- Understand the role of an officer in a criminal trial versus a civil trial
- Become sensitive to juries
- Understand the role of an expert witness

One of the primary rules of testifying in court is to present an acceptable appearance. The type of clothing worn by a traffic officer may vary depending on the desire of the particular court. Some areas prefer that an officer who normally works in uniform appear in uniform for court. Other locations prefer that the officer appear in civilian clothes. In either situation, the officer needs to remember that the expectation of the public is that he be exemplary in all things. He will often be judged on how he looks when appearing in court. If a uniform is to be worn, it is important to take the extra time to make sure that the brass and leather are polished and that the uniform is neatly pressed. If the officer needs a haircut, rather than put it off, it would be best to take care of that matter before appearing in court.

The one area that most frequently causes problems for officers testifying in court is the lack of preparation. It is likely to be several weeks or even months before the case will be heard, and the memory may pale slightly during that period and require refreshment. One of the best friends an officer has in his work is a notebook. On any arrest it is essential that the officer take the time to make individual notes that will refresh his memory when it comes time to testify. If a traffic citation is being contested, the officer will be well prepared if he can turn over his copy and on the reverse side find some fresh notes taken at the time while everything was current in his mind. Probably seeing the notes on the back of the citation will be enough to refresh the memory. If the case is of a more serious nature, there will be reports to review, and the information contained in the reports will only be of benefit if it is complete. An officer needs to have had the embarrassing experience of a lapse of memory or a lack of information while on the witness stand to truly appreciate the need for complete data.

If the matter is a felony trial, there will have been a preliminary hearing. During the preliminary hearing, a transcript was taken of everyone's testimony. The officer should specifically review the transcript of the preliminary hearing in order to recall exactly how he testified and be able to continue following that line of testimony. This is not to say that the officer would be untruthful the second time around, but, rather, it would be helpful to be as precise in repeating information as possible.

Defense attorneys will vary in their nature. No doubt the officer will encounter one or more in his career who will use badgering tactics in the hopes that he will rattle the officer on the witness stand and cause him to make a mistake or to appear unsure of himself. The success in this type of tactic quite often comes from the attorney having done his homework well and having researched the case more thoroughly than the officer. He is, therefore, in a better position to ask questions that the officer may not be prepared to answer.

In the matter of drunk driving arrests, there is one particular approach that has been successful for many defense attorneys. It deals with the issue of prejudice on the part of the officer.

The attorney will attempt to convince the jury that the officer had made up his mind, prior to stopping the defendant's vehicle, that the defendant was drunk. He will ask the officer if it is true that he had made this decision prior to stopping the car. If the officer denies the prejudice, the attorney will usually present questions that will infer the contrary. For instance, if the officer made a statement on the radio that he was stopping a possible drunk driver, the attorney will attack by suggesting that the officer, by making that statement, was convinced the driving behavior was caused by intoxication rather than sleepiness, illness, or defective steering, etc. It will be difficult for the officer to rebut this since he has only the option of answering questions with a yes or no answer most of the time. Hopefully, the prosecuting attorney will protect the officer from badgering questions by objecting at the appropriate time.

One way to absolutely avoid the type of attack previously mentioned in reference to drunk driving arrests is to make a habit of approaching a suspected drunk driver with a query of concern. If a vehicle is stopped that is weaving on the highway, it is true that the reason may be other than intoxication. Therefore, the officer can develop a habit of approaching the driver and asking the question, "Are you all right?" This procedure prefaces the initial contact with a concern for the welfare of the driver as opposed to a punitive inquiry. The officer will also find that there are people who are driving while sleepy or ill or who are having difficulty with their vehicle. It is a precautionary move to avoid a problem in court.

Some attorneys have practiced their abrasiveness to the point of almost guaranteeing that an officer will eventually explode on the stand when exposed to their particular type of innuendo during questioning. The officer who does this becomes his own worst enemy. If he manages to remain calm and to answer the questions carefully and factually, the attorney soon becomes the villian in the eyes of the jury and loses his effectiveness in this tactic.

The crime of perjury is a very serious offense and can have a lasting effect on a person's life. In the case of a police officer who "stretches the truth," it may ruin his career and even cause him to go to prison. The majority of police officers are honest people; however, there arises a temptation in every officer's career to embellish the truth in order to guarantee a conviction. Consider this a loud warning against such temptation. If the officer does not have sufficient evidence for a conviction, he should take the loss gracefully and learn from it. If he does not like the feeling of losing in court, he will probably improve his investigative techniques, record keeping, and testimony so that he will not lose as often in the future. Testifying in court can be the rewarding result of hard work. It can also become a nightmare if the officer is ill prepared or unsure of his facts.

The role of a police officer in a criminal case is to speak for the people in presenting evidence against a criminal. The officer is quite often the sole witness or at least a key witness, and his testimony is essential. It is important while preparing a case in the field, whether it be a traffic citation or a felony drunk driving, to remember that the matter will eventually end up before the court. This will hopefully provide motivation in carefully preparing the case from the very beginning. It may help to visualize just how to testify on various aspects of the case while conducting the investigation.

Many traffic matters, especially traffic accidents, will eventually be heard in civil court. This is because property damage or personal injury usually results, and one party is attempting to recover in a monetary way from the other. The officer may be subpoenaed by either party, and when he goes to court in a civil trial, he is the witness for whomever has supoenaed him. This is not to say that he should become a partial witness. Usually an attorney will discuss the testimony in advance of the court date and the officer will be familiar with what will be expected of him. He cannot, however, always expect the rebuttal that will come from the cross-examination by the other party's attorney.

Early in my career I was subpoenaed to civil court in the matter of an industrial injury. A serious injury had occurred to the plaintiff and he was in turn suing seven people. Consequently, there were seven defense attorneys who were particularly concerned with their own client's protection. Each question that the plaintiff's attorney asked me was objected to seven times, once by each defense attorney. It took quite a while for the judge to deal with each objection in turn, and to rule on them so that I might answer the question.

During my testimony, I made a minor error in recalling a measurement that I had visually taken at the scene. It seemed minor to me, but it was of great consequence to one of the defendants. Realizing my error, I approached the plaintiff's attorney in the hallway and notified him of the mistake. He said that it would be easy to correct the problem by asking me, on the stand, after the break, about the measurement again. This was done and I stated my error. There was a violent reaction from one of the defense attorneys who accused me of collusion with the plaintiff and who formally attempted to impeach my testimony. It was a frightening experience to a young officer who was used to only following the criminal court procedure, and I did not soon forget it.

If an officer is investigating a matter that he thinks may possibly go to civil litigation, he should begin to prepare himself for the civil aspect as well as the criminal. It will save him a headache at a future date.

In the case of a jury trial, the officer needs to become sensitive to the jury. These people are the representatives of the community who will judge guilt or innocence in the matter of a criminal case or assign blame and responsibility in a civil matter. They are usually ordinary people from all walks of life and have various experience with the police. Some of them will have no contact in their past with a police officer and have a limited basis for opinion. It is important that the officer present himself in his best manner at all times, but particularly in cases involving juries. When an attorney asks a question on the stand, the question is to ascertain information for the jury. Therefore, an officer who is aware will address his answer to the jury. Some attorneys will preface their questions by saying, "Officer, will you tell the jury . . ." Even if this is not said, it is still appropriate for the officer to remember that the jury is the group who must decide the issue and therefore, he must be sensitive to them and attentive to their needs in terms of information.

The rules of testimony change when they involve an expert

witness. An expert is a person who can qualify before the court to testify on his knowledge of a particular subject. If it is a matter involving firearms, a gunsmith may be qualified to convince the court that he is an expert in the matter of firearms. He can then present his opinion as opposed to the usual witness who may only state facts.

A traffic officer may develop the expertise to become qualified as an expert witness. This is usually in the category of speed determination from skidmarks. If an officer has aspirations of qualifying as an expert witness, he must prepare himself with careful deliberation. Usually the defense will provide its own "expert" who will possibly attempt to rebut the officer's opinion statements. Juries will usually consider the qualifications of both witnesses, but also juries are definitely affected by the manner and the sincerity of the witness. They will quite often brush aside long and meritorious qualifications and credentials to accept what they consider a more sincere and genuine answer.

It is important to be cautious when testifying as an expert in order to restrict answers to the realm of one's knowledge. It will be tempting sometimes for the officer to reach a little farther than he actually has expertise, and he may be burned badly by an opposing witness's testimony or by embarrassing questions from the attorney which he cannot answer. If he is well versed in his field of expertise, and it becomes readily apparent that his background and knowledge are solid, most defense attorneys will avoid challenging him because to do so would only reinforce his standing. This is a suggestion to be conservative in the beginning years of expert testimony if that is the officer's interest. Many years of traffic law enforcement experience do not automatically qualify an officer as an expert in the field of traffic. He must be specifically experienced in one particular aspect of the field and be prepared to present an adequate background and a clear knowledge of the subject.

It can be rewarding for an officer to add the scope of expert testimony to his experience. It is one area of reward which is available to the officer who specializes in traffic law enforcement.

APPENDIX

Structure 1. Traffic citation form used by the California Highway Patrol. It is also used as a legal complaint form in many courts.

Structure 2. Completed copy of a traffic citation.

Appendix

```
           LIGHT              CLEAR                WET
           MODERATE           CLOUDY               DRY
           HEAVY
CHP VEH - PKD ROLLING - STOPPED ON_____
DIR - N E S W - LANE  1  2  3  4  5  OTHER_____
CHP VEH NO._____YR. MAKE_____
DATE CALIB._____ | 30 | 40 | 50 | 60 | 65 | 70 | 80
BY_____  |    |    |    |    |    |    |
STOPPED BY    RED LITE,    SIREN,    HORN,    HAND
DEF - VEH - PKD ROLLING - STOPPED ON _____
DIR - N E S W - LANE  1  2  3  4  5  OTHER_____
STOPPED AT_____
DRIVER - OUT OF CAR          IN CAR
ATTITUDE: GOOD POOR BAD OTHER_____
PASSENGERS: SOLO_____RF_____MF_____RR_____
MR_____LR_____OTHER_____
CARS PASSED PASSING ON RT._____
DISTANCE OBSERVED_____
DISTANCE CHP VEH BEHIND_____
SPEAK ENGLISH?        YES         NO         FAIR
UNUSUAL CLOTHING?       , ACTIONS       , REMARKS
```

Structure 3. Reverse side of California Highway Patrol traffic citation.

CALIFORNIA HIGHWAY PATROL

NOTICE OF
PARKING - REGISTRATION
VIOLATION

B 336154

DATE	TIME	DAY OF WEEK
19	M	

REGISTERED OWNER OR LESSEE

ADDRESS (STREET OR ROAD)   CITY   ZIP CODE

VEHICLE LICENSE NO.   STATE

YEAR OF VEH.   MAKE   BODY STYLE   COLOR

WAS PARKED ON _____

AT OR NEAR _____

VIOLATIONS _____

THE TIME AND PLACE FIXED FOR APPEARANCE BY THE REGISTERED OWNER OR LESSEE OF SAID VEHICLE IS BEFORE THE JUDGE OF THE

☐ MUNICIPAL COURT
☐ JUSTICE COURT IN _____
                            (CITY OR TOWN)

AT _____
      (ADDRESS)   (ZIP CODE)

☐ ON THE _____ DAY OF _____ 19____ AT _____ M
☐ WITHIN ELEVEN DAYS
☐ OR YOU MAY APPEAR AT _____ P.M. ON _____
    TO ANSWER CHARGE OF VIOLATION (S) DESCRIBED ABOVE.

☐ MAY BE HANDLED BY MAIL   BAIL $

ISSUING OFFICER   I.D.   PERM. AREA

AREA	BEAT	SPECIAL	

CHP 267 (REV. 3-74) ℗f

Structure 4. Parking citation used by the California Highway Patrol.

CALIFORNIA HIGHWAY PATROL
NOTICE OF PARKING - REGISTRATION VIOLATION

B 336154

DATE	TIME	DAY OF WEEK
DEC. 7, 1977	6:30 PM	FRIDAY

REGISTERED OWNER OR LESSEE: RALPH ARMSTEAD
ADDRESS (STREET OR ROAD): 2109 BOSTON CT. CITY: ARCATA ZIP CODE: 95521
VEHICLE LICENSE NO.: VQL 829 STATE: CAL.
YEAR OF VEH.: 69 MAKE: OLDS. BODY STYLE: 2 DR. COLOR: GREEN

WAS PARKED ON: US 101
AT OR NEAR: TOMKINS HILL RD.
VIOLATIONS: 22504 CVC FAILURE TO PARK OFF OF THE ROADWAY

THE TIME AND PLACE FIXED FOR APPEARANCE BY THE REGISTERED OWNER OR LESSEE OF SAID VEHICLE IS BEFORE THE JUDGE OF THE

[X] MUNICIPAL COURT
[ ] JUSTICE COURT IN: EUREKA (CITY OR TOWN)

AT: COURTHOUSE (ADDRESS) 95501 (ZIP CODE)

[ ] ON THE _____ DAY OF _____ 19_____ AT _____ M
[X] WITHIN ELEVEN DAYS
[ ] OR YOU MAY APPEAR AT _____ P.M. ON _____
TO ANSWER CHARGE OF VIOLATION(S) DESCRIBED ABOVE.

[X] MAY BE HANDLED BY MAIL BAIL $ 10.00

ISSUING OFFICER: Backam I.D.: 3980 PERM. AREA: 125
AREA: 125 BEAT: 24 SPECIAL:

CHP 267 (REV. 3-74)

Structure 5. Completed example of California Highway Patrol Parking citation.

IMPORTANT
DRIVER'S LICENSE

You must bring your driver's license with you when you appear. If the address on your license is incorrect, have same corrected by the Department of Motor Vehicles. This applies to change of address on registration certificate also.

FAILURE TO APPEAR

Failure to appear at the time and place designated will result in further legal action against you.

See California Vehicle Code Sections 41102; 40513

WARNING

Vehicles registered other than in California may be impounded for repeated parking violations.

See California Vehicle Code Section 22651 (i)

IN ADDITION TO ANY FINE OR PENALTY THE COURT MAY IMPOSE, SATISFACTORY EVIDENCE THAT THE REGISTRATION VIOLATION HAS BEEN CORRECTED WILL BE REQUIRED BY THE COURT.

PROOF OF CORRECTION MAY BE OBTAINED AT OFFICES OF THE DEPARTMENT OF MOTOR VEHICLES OR CALIFORNIA HIGHWAY PATROL DURING NORMAL BUSINESS HOURS.

CERTIFICATE OF CORRECTION					
SECTION VIOLATED	SIGNATURE OF OFFICER OR EMPLOYEE CERTIFYING CORRECTION	I.D. NO.	AGENCY	DATE

Structure 6. Reverse side of the California Highway Patrol parking citation.

CALIFORNIA HIGHWAY PATROL
NOTICE OF VEHICLE CODE VIOLATION

| DATE 19 | TIME M | DAY OF WEEK |

NAME (FIRST, MIDDLE, LAST)

| RESIDENCE ADDRESS | CITY | ZIP CODE |

| BUSINESS ADDRESS | CITY | ZIP CODE |

| DRIVER'S LICENSE NO. | STATE | BIRTHDATE |

| SEX | HAIR | EYES | HEIGHT | WEIGHT |

| VEHICLE LICENSE NO. | STATE |

| YEAR OF VEH. | MAKE | BODY STYLE | COLOR |

REGISTERED OWNER OR LESSEE

| ADDRESS OF OWNER OR LESSEE | ZIP CODE |

LOCATION OF VIOLATION(S)

VIOLATION(S)

CC 8801094

SEAT BELT IN USE ☐ YES ☐ NO

I.D.   PERM. AREA

OFFICER

NOTICE CORRECT VIOLATION(S) IMMEDIATELY, RETURN THIS CARD WITH CERTIFICATION OR PROOF OF COMPLIANCE WITHIN 14 DAYS TO PATROL OFFICE SHOWN ON REVERSE SIDE.

I UNDERSTAND FAILURE TO COMPLY MAY RESULT IN COURT ACTION
X DRIVER'S SIGNATURE

FOR OFFICE USE ONLY

CHP FORM 281 (REV. 3-73)

Structure 7. This document is called a mechanical warning. It is often referred to as a "fix-it ticket," since proof of correction is all that is required of the driver.

150   *Traffic Law Enforcement*

CALIFORNIA HIGHWAY PATROL
NOTICE OF VEHICLE CODE VIOLATION

DATE	TIME	DAY OF WEEK
DEC. 7, 1977	8:30 P.M.	FRIDAY

NAME (FIRST, MIDDLE, LAST): DONALD D. TOLLIVER
RESIDENCE ADDRESS: 2917 FIRST AVE., **CITY:** SACRAMENTO **ZIP CODE:** 95814
BUSINESS ADDRESS: 1611 BROADWAY, **CITY:** SACRAMENTO **ZIP CODE:** 95814
DRIVER'S LICENSE NO.: G206271 **STATE:** CAL. **BIRTHDATE:** 6/11/42
SEX: M **HAIR:** BRN **EYES:** BLU **HEIGHT:** 5-11 **WEIGHT:** 165
VEHICLE LICENSE NO.: 411 AXS **STATE:** CAL.
YEAR OF VEH.: 76 **MAKE:** FORD **BODY STYLE:** 2DR. **COLOR:** BLUE
REGISTERED OWNER OR LESSEE: SAME AS DRIVER
ADDRESS OF OWNER OR LESSEE: **ZIP CODE:**

LOCATION OF VIOLATION(S): S/B WALNUT DR./CAMPTON RD.
VIOLATION(S): 24002 CVC VEHICLE NOT EQUIP. AS REQ'D: 1. DEFECTIVE TAIL LAMPS 2. DEFECTIVE STOP LAMPS 3. BALD RIGHT REAR TIRE

CC 880194

SEAT BELT IN USE: ☐ YES ☒ NO
OFFICER: D. Badham **I.D.:** 3980 **PERM. AREA:** 125

NOTICE CORRECT VIOLATION(S) IMMEDIATELY, RETURN THIS CARD WITH CERTIFICATION OR PROOF OF COMPLIANCE WITHIN 14 DAYS TO PATROL OFFICE SHOWN ON REVERSE SIDE.

I UNDERSTAND FAILURE TO COMPLY MAY RESULT IN COURT ACTION
☒ **DRIVER'S SIGNATURE:** Donald D. Tolliver

DRIVER'S INSTRUCTIONS ON BACK OF CARD

Structure 8. Completed example of the mehcanical warning.

Appendix 151

INSTRUCTIONS TO DRIVER-OWNER

This record may be cleared in the following manner:
1. Lamp and brake violations may be cleared by certification of an official Lamp or Brake Adjusting Station that the violations have been corrected. Card may then be mailed to the Patrol address indicated.
2. By submitting satisfactory proof of correction at a California Highway Patrol Office during normal business hours.
3. Registration and Driver's License violations may be cleared at offices of the Department of Motor Vehicles by an appropriate employee thereof, and the certified card mailed to the Patrol address indicated.
4. Pollution control device violations must be cleared by certification of an official Motor Vehicle Pollution Control Device Installation and Inspection Station.

— **VIOLATION CORRECTED** — DATE_____19____

OFFICIAL POLLUTION
CONTROL DEVICE, BRAKE
OR LAMP STATION_____

CERTIFIED BY_____DATE_____19____
(AUTHORIZED CHP OR DMV EMPLOYEE)

POST CARD

CALIFORNIA HIGHWAY PATROL
255 East Samoa Boulevard
Arcata, California 95521

PLACE
PROPER
POSTAGE
HERE

Structure 9. Reverse side of violator's copy of the warning citation used by the California Highway Patrol.

Structure 10. Arrest—Investigation Report used by the California Highway Patrol.

Appendix

Structure 11. Completed copy of California Highway Patrol Arrest — Investigation Report.

Structure 12. Reverse side of California Highway Patrol Arrest — Investigation Report.

Appendix

INTOXICATION INTERROGATION				
DO YOU KNOW OF ANYTHING MECHANICALLY WRONG WITH YOUR VEHICLE? DESCRIBE. ☐ YES ☒ NO			ARE YOU SICK OR INJURED? DESCRIBE. ☐ YES ☒ NO	
ARE YOU DIABETIC OR EPILEPTIC? ☐ YES ☒ NO	DO YOU TAKE INSULIN? (PILLS OR INJECTION) ☐ YES ☒ NO	DO YOU HAVE ANY PHYSICAL DEFECTS? DESCRIBE. (FEET, LEGS, ANKLES OR HIPS) ☐ YES ☒ NO		
WHEN DID YOU LAST SLEEP? **LAST NIGHT**	HOW LONG? **7 HRS.**	WHEN DID YOU LAST EAT? **DINNER, TONITE**	DESCRIBE **STEAK, BAKED POTATO**	
WERE YOU DRIVING THE VEHICLE? ☒ YES ☐ NO ☐ N/A	IF NO, WHO?		WHERE DID YOU START DRIVING? **EUREKA**	WHERE WERE YOU GOING? **SAN FRANCISCO**
WHERE ARE YOU NOW? **OAKLAND?**	WHAT HAVE YOU BEEN DRINKING? **BOURBON**		HOW MUCH? **ABOUT 4**	TIME STARTED **6PM** / TIME STOPPED **9PM**
WHERE WERE YOU DRINKING? **RED LION BAR**		DO YOU FEEL THE EFFECTS OF THE DRINKS? DESCRIBE. ☐ YES ☒ NO		
DID YOU BUMP YOUR HEAD? ☐ YES ☒ NO	HAVE YOU BEEN DRINKING SINCE THE ACCIDENT? ☐ YES ☒ N/A		WHAT? —	HOW MUCH? —
ARE YOU UNDER CARE OF DOCTOR OR DENTIST? ☒ YES ☐ NO	IF YES, NAME AND ADDRESS **DR. ARNDT, M.D., SAN FRANCISCO**			
HAVE YOU TAKEN ANY MEDICINE OR DRUGS? ☒ YES ☐ NO	IF YES, WHAT **ALLERGY PILLS**		HOW MUCH? **2**	TIME OF LAST DOSAGE **8PM**
DO YOU FEEL THE EFFECTS OF THE DRUGS? DESCRIBE. **NO**				

FIELD SOBRIETY TEST – ALCOHOL/DRUGS			
BREATH ODOR OF ALCOHOL ☐ STRONG ☒ MOD ☐ WEAK	GLASSES/LENSES ☐ YES ☒ NO	HEEL TO TOE/WALKING LINE TEST △ L. FOOT ○ R. FOOT	

ATTITUDE
COOPERATIVE

EYES
RED, WATERY, SLOW PUPIL REACTION

SPEECH
SLURRED, DIFFICULT TO UNDERSTAND

CLOTHING WORN/CONDITION AND DESCRIPTION
BROWN SUIT, TAN SHIRT, BROWN TIE, BROWN WING TIP SHOES

DESCRIBE TEST LOCATION, SURFACE, WEATHER AND LIGHTING
ASPHALT PAVED SHOULDER, SMOOTH, LEVEL – CLEAR, DRY – HEADLIGHTS

IDENTIFY AND DESCRIBE EACH TEST GIVEN
SIMPLE BALANCE: FEET TOGETHER, HEAD BACK, EYES CLOSED.
JOHNSON SWAYED IN AN APPROX. 6-8" ARC.
STANDING ON ONE FOOT: UNABLE TO PERFORM.
FINGER TO NOSE: WITH EYES CLOSED, TOUCH TIP ON ON COMMAND
WITH SPECIFIED INDEX FINGER. RT. HAND – TOUCHED UPPER LIP
LEFT HAND – TOUCHED BRIDGE OF THE NOSE.
COUNT ON FINGERS: "1234 – 4231, OOPS, 4123 – 3421, OOPS".
RECITE ALPHABET: "A, B, C, D, E, G, L, M, N, P, U, X, Y, Z."

IMPLIED CONSENT 13353 V.C.				
YOU ARE REQUIRED BY STATE LAW TO SUBMIT TO A CHEMICAL TEST TO DETERMINE THE ALCOHOLIC CONTENT OF YOUR BLOOD. YOU HAVE A CHOICE OF WHETHER THE TEST IS TO BE OF YOUR BLOOD, BREATH OR URINE. IF YOU REFUSE TO SUBMIT TO A TEST OR FAIL TO COMPLETE A TEST YOUR DRIVING PRIVILEGE WILL BE SUSPENDED FOR A PERIOD OF SIX MONTHS. YOU DO NOT HAVE THE RIGHT TO TALK TO AN ATTORNEY OR TO HAVE AN ATTORNEY PRESENT BEFORE STATING WHETHER YOU WILL SUBMIT TO A TEST, BEFORE DECIDING WHICH TEST TO TAKE, OR DURING THE ADMINISTRATION OF THE TEST CHOSEN.				
THE ABOVE STATEMENT WAS READ TO THE ARRESTEE BY: *A.J. Bashan*			I.D. **3980**	TIME **2345**
☒ BLOOD ☐ BREATH ☐ URINE ☐ DL 367 COMPLETED ☐ REFUSED	TIME 1. **2346** 2.	I.D. OF SAMPLE **37A**	RESULTS, IF AVAILABLE	DISPOSITION OF SAMPLE **RETAINED BY TECH.**
LOCATION WHERE TEST CONDUCTED **HUMBOLDT COUNTY JAIL**		NAME AND TITLE OF PERSON GIVING TEST OR TAKING SAMPLE **A.L. BREWSTER, LAB. TECH.**		

Structure 13. Completed example of reverse side of California Highway Patrol Arrest – Investigation Report.

Structure 14. Supplemental/Narrative form used by the California Highway Patrol.

SUPPLEMENTAL/NARRATIVE (Check one)	DATE OF ORIGINAL INCIDENT 1 23 78 MO. DAY YR.	TIME (2400) 2305	NCIC NUMBER	OFFICER I.D. 3980	NUMBER M61275	PAGE 3
☐ NARRATIVE CONTINUATION TRAFFIC COLLISION REPORT (CHP 555 OR 555-01) ☐ SUPPLEMENTAL TRAFFIC COLLISION REPORT (CHP 555 OR 555-01) ☒ OTHER: DWI ARREST	LOCATION/SUBJECT				CITATION NUMBER W137526	
					BEAT 18	
	CITY/COUNTY				REPORTING DISTRICT	

P.C. TO ARREST: (CONT.) SUBJ.'S SHIRTTAIL HANGING OUT OF HIS TROUSERS IN BACK. OTHER CLOTHING DISARRANGED. PUPIL REACTION VERY SLOW IN BOTH EYES WHEN EXPOSED TO FLASHLIGHT. DUE TO SUBJ. JOHNSON'S DRIVING, ODOR OF LIQUOR ABOUT HIS PERSON, UNSTEADY BALANCE, GENERAL APPEARANCE AND DEMEANOR AS WELL AS POOR RESULTS FROM FST, I FORMED THE OPINION THAT MR. JOHNSON WAS INTOXICATED. THE CAUSE OF INTOXICATION APPEARED TO BE ALCOHOLIC BEVERAGE (PARTIALLY EMPTY PINT BOTTLE OF FOUR ROSES BOURBON ON THE FLOORBOARD BY THE DRIVERS DOOR, OBS. BY ME WHEN HE EXITED FROM THE VEH.).
MR. JOHNSON WAS PLACED UNDER ARREST AND HANDCUFFED AT 2315 HRS.

P.C. TO SEARCH: SUBJ. JOHNSON'S CLOTHING WAS SEARCHED AT THE TIME OF ARREST BY ME AND A PLASTIC PILL BOTTLE WAS FOUND CONTAINING 3 YELLOW CAPSULS. HE STATED THAT THESE WERE MEDECATION FOR ALLERGY PRESCRIBED BY DR. ARNDT, M.D., IN SAN FRANCISCO. THE CAPSULS HAVE FORWARDED TO THE HUMBOLDT LAB FOR ANALYSIS. THE FOUR ROSES BOTTLE, MENTIONED ABOVE, WAS SEIZED. ADDITIONALLY, THE INTERIOR OF THE VEHICLE WAS SEARCHED FOR OTHER EVIDENCE OR CONTRABAND WITH NEGATIVE RESULTS.
A BLOOD SAMPLE WAS WITHDRAWN FROM SUBJ. JOHNSON'S RT. INNER ELBOW BY LAB TECH. AT THE COUNTY JAIL FOR THE PURPOSE OF DETERMINING A B/A LEVEL.
THE SEARCH OF JOHNSON'S CLOTHING AND VEHICLE, AND THE BLOOD SAMPLE COLLECTION WERE BASED ON FACTS INCIDENTAL TO THE ARREST.

Structure 15. Completed copy of Supplemental/Narrative form.

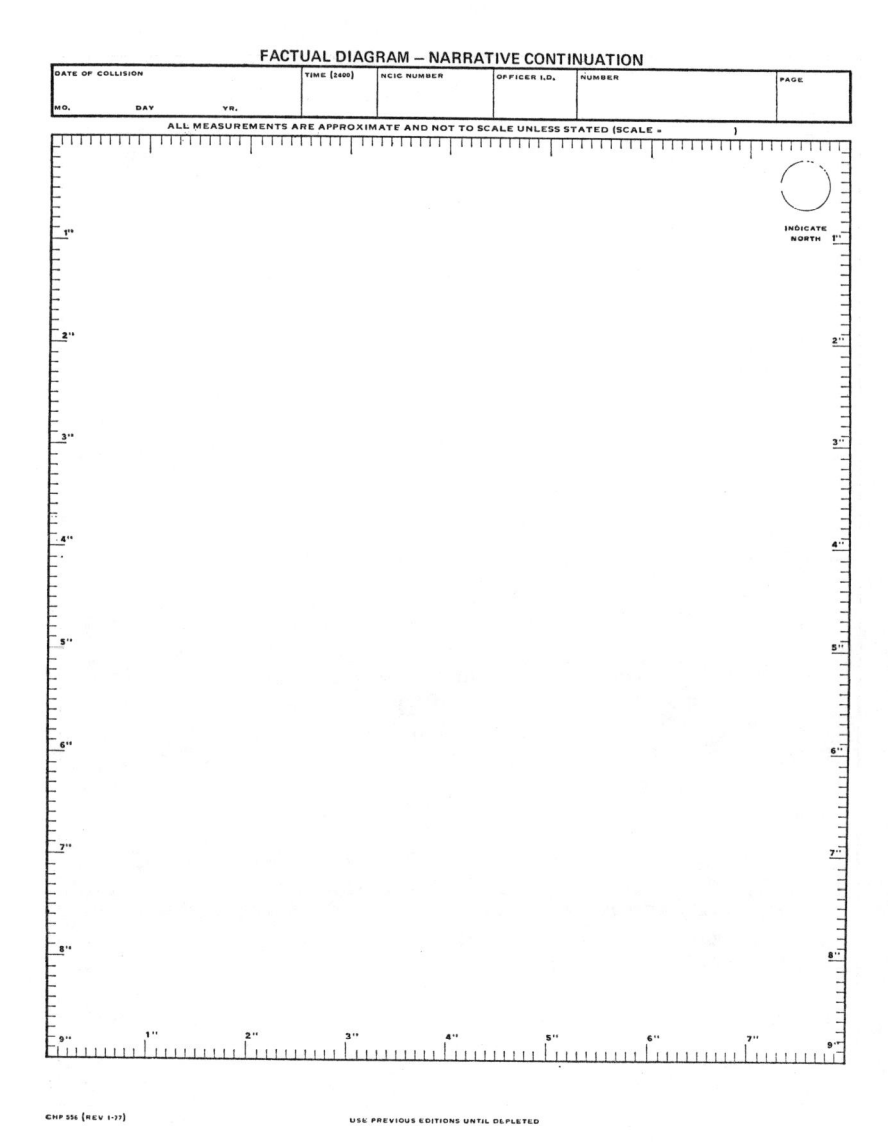

Structure 16. Reverse side of Supplemental/Narrative form.

Appendix 159

Structure 17. Stolen/Embezzled Vehicles, Plate(s) Report used by the California Highway Patrol.

Structure 18. Abandoned, Impounded, Recovered, Stored or Released Vehicle Report used by the California Highway Patrol.

INDEX

A
accident, 3, 79
Accident Probability Chart, 3
accident (traffic), 3
air brakes, 3, 60
alcohol, 4, 103, 104, 105
alcoholic, 113
alley, 4
amphetamines, 114
approach, 38, 39, 40
arrest, 4, 117, 118, 119
arrest report, Chap. 14
authorized emergency vehicle, 4
axle, 4

B
backup unit, 41, 94
balance, 44, 45
barbiturates, 114
basic speed law, 65
bicycle, 4
blood/alcohol level, 4, 123
blood sample, 122, 123
body fluids, 123, 124
brake lights, 57
brakes, 58, 60
breath analysis, 123
bus, 4
business district, 4

C
calibration, 68
camper, 4
capability, 28
carbon monoxide, 59
chemical test, 123, 124
cocaine, 115
communication, 28
confidence, 28
confinement, 28, 29
control, 28, 29
counterfeit documents, 55

court testimony, Chap. 15
cover, 43, 92
cross examination, 138
crosswalk, 5, 82
custody, 5

D
darkness, 5
directing traffic, 17-25
dispatcher, 5
drinking, 103, 104
driver, 5
driver's license, 5, 52, 53, 54, 61
drug, 5
drunk, 5
D.W.I., 5

E
electric fifth wheel, 68
emergency, 5
emergency stopping system, 60, 61
emergency vehicle, 5
emergency warning lamps, 29, 30, 31, 72, 73, 83
enforcement policy, 15
equipment inspection, 56-63
essential parts, 5
exhaust system, 59
expert witness, 140

F
feet per second, 66
felony stops, Chap. 11
fender, 6
field sobriety test, 106, 107, 108, 109, 110, 111
fifth wheel, 6, 62
fixed post, 6
flammable liquid, 6
flare pattern, 6
following too closely, 88
freeway, 6
fusee, 6

G

generalist, 12
green signal, 82

H

halo effect, 13, 72
handcuffs, 96
hashish, 115
heroin, 115
high speed pursuit, 73
highway, 6
horn, 57
house car, 6
hunter instinct, 80
hydraulic brakes, 58

I

identification documents, Chap. 6
illegal, 6
impeding traffic, 86
impound, 121, 122
initial contact, 48
injury, 6
inspection, 56-63
intersection, 7
intoxicated driver, 117, 121, 124, 129, 137
intoxication, 7, 105, 106, 112
investigation, 7

J

jurisdiction, 7
jury trial, 139

L

lamp lenses, 58
lecture, 49
lights, 57, 59
limit line, 7, 82
local authorities, 7
LSD, 115

M

male driver, 49
mandatory, 7
marijuana, 115
maximum speed limit, 64
may, 7
morphine, 115
motor cycle, 7

motor vehicle, 7
muffler system, 7, 59
must, 8

N

narrative, 130
notebook, 136

O

odometer, 8, 68, 69, 70
officer, 8
official traffic control device, 8
official traffic control signal, 8
opiate, 115

P

pacing speed, 67, 70
park or parking, 8, 122
parking brake, 58
passengers, 119
passing, 86, 87
patrol, 80, 81
patrol car, 71, 89, 97
pedestrian, 8
pedestrian signals, 83
perjury, 137, 138
personal appearance, 135
pneumatic tire, 8
position, 42, 44, 45
power brakes, 8
power symbol, 76, 77
pressure gauge, 60
private road, 8
probability, 11
probability chart, 3, 14, 15, 16
probable cause, 131, 132
public address system, 83, 92, 96
pupil reaction, 112
pursuit policy, 74, 75

Q

questioning, 128, 129

R

radar, 8, 67
reaction time, 88
reconstructed vehicle, 8
red signal, 82
registered owner, 9

Index

registration, 9
residential district, 9
right-of-way, 9, 84
roadblock, 96, 97
roadway, 9
routine stop, 36

S

salvage switch, 54
search, 120, 132, 133
semitrailer, 9
sidewalk, 9
single control, 60
Sir Robert Peel, 51
siren, 9, 31, 72, 73, 89
siren hypnosis, 78
slow vehicles, 86
specially constructed vehicle, 9
speed, Chap. 8
speed calibration, 68
speed conversion, 66
speed trap, 9, 12
speedometer, 9, 67
stance, 44, 45
stop signs, 83
synergistic effect, 9

T

tires, 59
title, 10
touch, 42
tow truck, 10

traffic, 10
traffic citation, 10
traffic collision, 10
traffic officer, 10
traffic safety, 11
traffic stops, 10, 26, Chap. 3
traffic supervision, 11
truck brakes, 60
turn signals, 57
turning movements, 85, 86

U

under the influence, 10
urinalysis, 123

V

vehicle, 10
vehicle equipment inspection, 56-63
vehicle motion, 10
vehicle storage, 120
vehicular crossing, 10
videotape, 124, 125
VIN, 10, 54, 128

W

warning device, 60
whistle, 18-19
windshield wipers, 57
witness, 138

Y

yield sign, 84